I0128615

**Rejimon Kuttappan** is a migrant rights defender and an independent journalist. He was Chief Reporter for *Times of Oman*, one of the leading English dailies in Oman, till 2017. In April 2017, he was deported by the government of Oman for exposing the human trafficking of South Asian women domestic workers and modern-day slavery in the Arab Gulf through news stories published in the *Times of Oman*. Following that, he joined Equidem Research and Consulting, a specialist human and labour rights consultancy, as an India-Arab Gulf Senior Investigator.

Rejimon continues to be a regular contributor for Thomson Reuters Foundation, *Middle East Eye*, *Migrant Rights*, *Equal Times*, *Caravan*, wire.in, *The Lede*, *The News Minute* and various other news outlets. He writes on workers' rights, the struggles of Dalits and tribals, challenges faced by manual scavengers, and marginalized people in Kerala. He is also an ILO-Panos fellow on Labour Migration and an advisor for the Ethical Journalism Network. He has been published in an anthology, *Uncertain Journeys: Labour Migration from South Asia*, by Speaking Tiger (2018).

Rejimon belongs to a Dalit community in Kerala called Panans. They were historically ballad singers, reciting heroic acts by great warriors and kings. By telling the stories of the heroic fishermen who saved thousands of lives during the century's worst floods in this book, Rejimon believes that he is carrying on their storytelling legacy.

Rejimon now lives in Kerala and can be followed @rejitweets. He can be contacted at reji.news@gmail.com

## Praise for *Rowing Between the Rooftops*

'In *Rowing Between the Rooftops*, Rejimon Kuttapan brings to life the heroic, life-saving efforts, made by the fishing community of Kerala, particularly those from Thiruvananthapuram, at the height of the devastating floods that held the state of Kerala hostage in August 2018. Rejimon writes in a highly readable manner that brings their heroism to life. Each page, filled with heart-warming anecdotes of the valour of our coastal communities, provides a reflection of the selfless spirit that animates this community, whose members are well deserving of the highest praise and admiration from a grateful society. A work to cherish!'

—Dr Shashi Tharoor, M.P.

# Rowing Between the Rooftops

## The Heroic Fishermen of the Kerala Floods

REJIMON KUTTAPPAN

SPEAKING
**TIGER**

SPEAKING TIGER PUBLISHING PVT. LTD
4381/4, Ansari Road, Daryaganj
New Delhi 110002

First published in paperback by Speaking Tiger 2019

Copyright © Rejimon Kuttappan 2019

ISBN: 978-93-89231-18-2
eISBN: 978-93-88326-83-4

10 9 8 7 6 5 4 3 2 1

The moral right of the author has been asserted.

All rights reserved.
No part of this publication may be reproduced, transmitted,
or stored in a retrieval system, in any form or by
any means, electronic, mechanical, photocopying,
recording or otherwise, without the prior
permission of the publisher.

This book is sold subject to the condition that it shall not,
by way of trade or otherwise, be lent, resold, hired out,
or otherwise circulated, without the publisher's
prior consent in any form of binding or cover
other than that in which it is published.

*Dedicated to my father,*
*a great person who toiled even in sweatshops*
*to give me a decent education.*
*Unfortunately, he could not see my first book.*

# CONTENTS

# INTRODUCTION

In the South Indian state of Kerala, the fishermen along the coastline are known for their exemplary bravery. Although their actions are tied to a rich history, much of it has not been recorded, and the current generation had not witnessed examples of their heroism. All this changed in August 2018, when the worst floods of the century hit Central Kerala, and fishermen from all over the coast risked their lives, their boats—the only source of livelihood for many—and their health and strength to rescue thousands of stranded flood victims.

These fishermen ignored the heavy downpours during the rescue operations, steering their boats while soaked to the skin and on empty stomachs. They had to navigate the wild flood waters with their treacherous undercurrents, with their boats repeatedly catching on the rooftops of submerged houses. They had to dive deep into the dirty waters, ignoring the chances of contracting diseases and sustaining injuries. Many had to dock their boats on the second floor of the marooned houses and climb into the building to find the stranded people. Sometimes, they had to carry the rescued people out on their shoulders, or tie them to their own bodies and slide down a rope into the boat. When they had the gear, these fishermen shared their life jackets with the people they rescued. When the boats were filling up, some of them swam alongside, so that more people could be rescued on each trip.

Some of them had to hold on to power supply lines, hoping that they weren't carrying live current, in order to steer the boat or keep it afloat. Others encountered venomous snakes swimming in the flood water and even had to pick them up with their bare hands to fling them far away and save the whole boat.

While some imply that the fishermen jumped into action without thinking of the consequences, others say that they did so because they are simply unbothered by the possibility of loss. They are often seen as an innocent lot who will trust anyone who recognizes, respects and loves them, even laying down their lives, if needed. But when I went to the Thiruvananthapuram coast and asked the fishermen themselves why they are so willing to ignore all risks, they answered with a smile. After some prodding, they told me that they have ignored risks to save others' lives and protect their nation in the past, they continue to do so now, and will do the same in the future as well.

As Mini Mohan, a sociologist in Thiruvananthapuram, explains, people in Kerala are aware of the courage of these fishermen through blurred stories passed on from generation to generation. The final chapter of this book, 'A History of Heroism', explores this history, telling how the forefathers of these fishermen risked their lives to pledge allegiance to the rulers of Travancore in the sixteenth century, and how they were instrumental in repelling the Dutch naval invasion along the Colachel coast in the eighteenth century.

However, now people all over the world have seen the unparalleled bravery of the Kerala fishermen with their own eyes.

*

Even before the government thought of seeking the help of the fishermen, these heroes of the Thiruvananthapuram coast had rushed to the flooded areas, ignoring the risks, as usual. In fact, it can be argued that government officials only realized that the fishermen could rescue people from marooned houses after the first few boats had already reached the flooded areas and they had started saving lives. Government statistics reveal that fishermen rescued some 65,000 people from flood-hit areas, mainly in Chengannur and other parts of Central Travancore. In contrast, trained Indian Army and Navy personnel could only rescue around 8,000 people.

Following a week-long rescue operation, the fishermen returned home to a heroic welcome. They were christened Kerala's Own Navy, and some even compared them to Superman and Batman. But none of the fishermen who had been at the scene of action knew that they were being compared to superheroes. Many of them had travelled 200 kilometres from their homes to the flood-hit areas without even telling their near and dear ones.

According to Johny Chekkitta, one of the fishermen who sprang into action with his six friends, hiring both a boat and a truck to transport it long before the government sought their help, doing so would have held them back. 'We may be courageous, we may not think of risks, but our family members do,' he said. 'We are the sole breadwinners of the family. If something happens to us, then they will be left alone and helpless. No one would take care of them even if we lay down our life in the rescue missions. This is Kerala. Our sacrifice will be on the news for a few days, but soon, when something else pops up, we will be forgotten. The most that we can expect is an annual remembrance. That's it. Will that help our wives and kids to buy rice?

'In fact, they know what to expect better than us. They think of the future, and we ignorant men think of today only....'

Johny's matter-of-fact acceptance of the fickleness of the world exemplifies why this book is needed at this time. It tells the stories of these men who saved the lives of Keralites—and that of the struggles that they face now. By the time I had finished interviewing them for this book, almost three months after the flood, these Supermen and Batmen were already forgotten. Some of them had been garlanded and given plaques and certificates of appreciation, but while visiting their homes, I found that the plaques in the showcases were already losing their shine. Almost all the erstwhile superheroes were struggling to find enough work to earn at least Rs 1,000 a week for survival. Nothing much has been done to help rebuild their boats or to compensate for their losses.

If the heroic acts of these fishermen are not written

about and shared, then, as in the past, only unclear stories will remain. And eventually, they will be forgotten.

\*

According to the Kerala fisheries minister, J. Mercykutty Amma, fishermen in 669 mechanized country boats rescued a total of 65,000 people, braving the torrential rains and floods. In Chengannur alone, about 70 per cent of the total number of people trapped were rescued by local fishermen who had to work in harsh weather throughout the operations.

The fisheries department resolved to field the fishermen for rescue operations on August 15, when the state started experiencing unusually heavy rains and floods. In order to do so, announcements were made over microphones in coastal areas, especially in the south, urging fishermen to launch rescue operations in the flooded inland areas. The local member of the legislative assembly (MLA) of Chengannur, Saji M. Cherian, even wept live on television, while pleading for help from the fishermen and other rescue teams, fearing that any delay could result in the loss of hundreds of lives.

Fishermen responded and came from far and

near, transporting their mechanized country boats in trucks seized by the government for the purpose, or hired through informal networks by the fishermen themselves. Churches in the southern coastal areas also played a vital role in mobilizing and helping the fishermen to arrange boats and transport to Chengannur to rescue stranded people. Many of those who had ventured into the sea for fishing were also called back and sent for rescue operations in the worst flood that Kerala had experienced in almost a century.

*

In an ordinary year, Kerala witnesses an average annual precipitation of about 3,000 mm. Rainfall in the state is controlled by the South-west and North-east monsoons. About 90 per cent of it occurs during the six monsoon months.

The high intensity storms prevailing during the monsoon months result in heavy discharges into all the rivers. The continuous and heavy precipitation that occurs in the steep and undulating terrain also finds its way into the main rivers through innumerable streams and water courses.

However, this year, Kerala experienced an

abnormally high level of rainfall from June 1 to August 29. This resulted in severe flooding in thirteen out of the fourteen districts in the state. Indian meteorological data shows that Kerala received 2,346.6 mm of rainfall from June 1 to August 19, 2018, in contrast to an expected 1,649.5 mm. This was about 42 per cent above the normal. Further, over the previous months, the rainfall over Kerala was 15 per cent above normal in June, 18 per cent higher in July, and a staggering 164 per cent higher between 1 and 19 August.

The water levels in several reservoirs were almost near their full capacities due to continuous rainfall from June 1. Thirty-five out of the fifty-four dams within the state were opened, for the first time in history. All five overflow gates of the Idukki Dam were opened at the same time, for the first time in twenty-six years. Water was released from several dams due to heavy rainfall in their catchment areas.

All fourteen districts in the state were placed on red alert. Approximately 500 people died and at least 1.5 million people had to be evacuated, mainly from Chengannur, Pandanad, Edanad, Aranmula, Kozhencherry, Ayiroor, Ranni, Pandalam, Kuttanad, Aluva, Chalakudy, N. Paravur, Chendamangalam, Eloor and a few places in Vypin Island. Heavy rains in Wayanad and Idukki caused severe landslides and left the hilly districts isolated.

The rainfall recorded during August 15-17 was comparable to the worst deluge faced in Kerala's records, known as the Great Flood.

*

In 1924*, the state had witnessed unprecedented flooding in almost all rivers of Kerala. The rainstorm of July 16-18, 1924 was caused by the South-west monsoon. The centre of this three-day rainstorm was located at Munnar, which recorded a rainfall of 897 mm in three days. Historian Meenu Jacob has noted in her article, '1924 flood of Travancore: A literary representation', that 'the significance of the flood was such that many old people used to anchor their memories in relation to it.' According to Jacob, events were reckoned as having occurred before, during or after the Great Flood.

Although the rainfall recorded in 1924 was far less, at 650 mm, in comparison to that received in 2018,

---

*The flood occurred in 1924 according to the Gregorian Calendar. However, as Kerala followed the Malayalam Calendar according to which it was 1099 at the time, the flood is called Thonnootti Onpathile Vellapokkam (flood of 99) and the Great Flood.

the impact of the deluge was no less. The torrential downpour caused the hill once known as Karinthiri to erode completely, and left the town of Munnar submerged. While official records are not available, the death toll of the Great Flood is believed to be around 1,000.

*Deepika*, the century-old Malayalam newspaper in Kerala, quoted several accounts by local correspondents about the Great Flood in its story of 24 July, 1994. They state that 'Ernakulam, Ponjikkara, Venduruthi, Njarakkal, took only a few hours to reach ocean-level'; 'the Broadway grounds in Ernakulam became an ocean' and 'very quickly boats conquered the streets of Ernakulam'. Amid reports of bridges being washed away, and transport being disrupted, 'the rail bridges at Chovvara, Edappally, Aluva, Chalakkudy had water flowing over them that could let a boat pass through'. They added that 'all high places on land were brimming with refugees', and that 8,000 refugees had gathered in 'Thiruvalla, Tirumoolapuram, Tookalsseri in two days'.

Bodies were seen floating and 'water rose up to three feet in the night and the salt and sugar stocked in Travancore's main trading centre of Alappuzha all dissolved and disappeared'. Many refugee camps were flooded, the reports said. At Manimala, Mundakkayom, 'houses were tied to trees with ropes' and '150 buildings floated by in two hours'. Accounts also talked about 'men and elephants flowing by', of 'carcasses of elephants'; 'a live tiger', and a leopard being washed down from the forests.

There is a widespread consensus among the older generation of Kerala that a breach of the Mullaperiyar Dam had prompted the floods. The reported breach had occurred just twenty-nine years after the dam was built. At the time, there were said to be no other dams in the region, implying that no other cause of such destructive floods was considered. When it comes to the 2018 flood, the Central Water Commission's report has revealed that the dams in Kerala neither added to the flood nor helped to reduce the floodwaters, as most of them were already at Full Reservoir Level (FRL) or very close to FRL on August 14, 2018, following higher than normal rainfall in the previous months. The report adds that the release from reservoirs had only a minor role in flood augmentation, as the released volumes from the reservoirs were almost like inflow volumes.

An interesting oral account from 1924 reveals that the flood entered the area around the Siva Temple at

Vaikom, even while the historic Vaikom Satyagraha (1924-25), a pre-Independence movement for the entry of all classes of people in the public roads surrounding the temple, was going on. The satyagrahis chose to continue their struggle, even though 'only their necks could be seen above the water level'.

The disastrous rains had their most severe impact on Travancore, which was transformed into a massive swamp during the few weeks when it kept pouring. Other areas of Kerala were also affected, including Trichur, Ernakulam, Idukki, Kottayam and the road leading up to Munnar. These were the same areas affected in the 2018 floods.

The Travancore government was swift to start relief work as soon as the crisis set in. By August 1924, thousands of refugees were in relief centres in Alappuzha, Kottayam, Ambalapuzha, Changanassery and many such places where there are camps functioning for the same purpose today. A Flood Relief Committee was set up by the government. Devan T. Raghavaiah, a civil servant deputed by the Madras Presidency, played an important role in the relief work, sending in large amounts of money to areas which were affected by the floods.

Further, after taking account of the monumental

loss incurred in agriculture, the government announced that in the worst affected regions, taxes would be remitted for that financial year. A sum of Rs 400,000 was also set aside to provide agricultural loans. The forest department was issued orders to supply free bamboo and other housing material to provide provisional residential arrangements for the poor. The government also set aside a housing reconstruction fund and took several measures to ensure that the stability of food prices was maintained.

Meanwhile, Mahatma Gandhi outlined the severity of the flood in a series of articles. In one such piece on August 3, 1924, he wrote, 'The havoc in Malabar is like a fire in the sea and it is beyond the means of any private organization to relieve the people's suffering'. In another article written on August 14, 1924, Gandhi observed, 'The floods in the Southern Presidency are so vast in their magnitude that imagination refuses to picture them. They demonstrate man's helplessness. Fruits of years of patient toil have been swept away in a moment. Help seems almost a mockery'. Stating that 'the damage is too vast for sporadic or isolated effort' Gandhi prescribed setting up 'some agency that would command universal confidence to handle the work of relief'. Appealing for relief from all quarters, he observed 'None should ask how much money would be needed' and affirmed that '"The more the merrier" is the rule which applies here.'

\*

Unfortunately, the ugly wrangling for relief funds in the aftermath of the 2018 floods shows that Gandhi's words go unheeded. The state government estimated a loss of about Rs 40,000 crores and has been scrambling to raise funds to rebuild a new Kerala. On September 25, 2018, the Kerala government had sought a special grant of Rs 5,000 crore from the centre for livelihood development in the flood-ravaged state. Chief Minister Pinarayi Vijayan submitted a memorandum listing the devastation in the state, rehabilitation works done and the assistance required for rebuilding Kerala after the deluge. While mentioning that around 700 families are still living in camps, the chief minister said that the disaster has affected 80 per cent of the state's population.

The state has sought to hike the current debt limit of 3.5 per cent of the Gross State Domestic Product (GSDP) to 4.5 per cent for the financial year 2018-19. Vijayan has also sought a hike of 10 per cent in assistance from central schemes, saying it will generate Rs 10,000 crore of additional aid for the state.

After the review, the Prime Minister announced financial assistance of Rs 500 crore to the state. This was in addition to Rs 100 crore announced by the Home Minister. He also assured the state government that relief materials including food grains, medicines etc would be provided, as requested.

Both the Prime Minister and Chief Minister praised the role that the fishermen played in rescue and relief efforts after the flood. Unfortunately, the fishermen cannot bask in their warm words when so many things remain to be done to improve their lives: they are continuing to repay loans taken for boats that were damaged in the rescue efforts and they need to find money for educating their children, buying medicines and building houses. With climate change, greater numbers of deadly floods and cyclones, and increasing coastal erosion affecting their livelihoods, many fishermen know all too well how precarious their lives have become.

*

According to the fishermen on the Thiruvananthapuram coast, the current precarity of their lives has been felt since Cyclone Ockhi passed through the area on November 29, 2017. In a shocking blow, eighty-nine fishermen were killed and 143 went missing within a matter of days, and the death toll continued to rise. Even one year later, when I met them in November 2018, those who had lost their kin to the disaster were finding it hard to make ends meet, while those who made it back alive have still not overcome the mental torture they went through.

Twenty-nine-year-old Selin Lorence, who lost her husband in the cyclone, told me that her husband had not been keen to go fishing on November 29, but as relatives and friends were ready to go, he also joined them. Lorence Peter, Selin's husband, was among the hundreds of fishermen who either went missing or were killed in the Indian Ocean.

'Despite hearing stories of casualties, I was hoping he would return. But on the evening of December 3, 2017, while we were running from the shore for shelter having heard tsunami rumours, relatives told me he was dead,' Selin said. 'I still remember, it was raining and we were all struggling to run to higher ground. My younger boy, who was just four months old, was in my arms covered with a cloth and my elder daughter was running with me. I felt a strange pain in my chest. I could hear my daughter cry, but I was unable to hold her.'

A year has passed and she is still struggling to make ends meet: 'Life is hell. I have to take care of my young children and old mother. I haven't found a job yet. And, even if I do, I can't leave my mentally ill mother with my young children.' She is trying to run the household with the Rs 14,000 she gets as monthly interest on the Rs 20 lakh deposited as compensation for Cyclone Ockhi in the state treasury by the government. 'It is very difficult to manage the expenses and repay the loan we took to buy the house we live in. The government is holding back the compensation and just releasing the interest, which is quite worrying,' she said.

Peter wasn't the only one this family lost. Kochappa, Selin's grandfather, saw eight deaths in his family that day.

Even those who were rescued from the sea are struggling to make ends meet. Lorence Bernard, from Poonthura in Thiruvananthapuram, had gone fishing with four friends, but he was the only one to make it back to the shore alive—that too after five days. During those five days of being awash in the ocean, the cyclone injured him so badly that, even a year later, he can't stand up without help.

'The families of those who had gone missing or died

got good compensation. All I got was Rs 25,000, and that too in three instalments. My physical condition doesn't allow me to stand up straight. Even if I was physically fit, those five days alone in the sea, when I saw my friends drown and faced the fury of the cyclone, have left me mentally unfit,' Bernard said.

*

Father Eugene H. Pereira from the Latin Catholic Church Bishop House said Ockhi forced fishermen who had previously owned their own boats to become daily wagers. 'The majority of them are struggling. Within a week, they all became daily wagers,' says Fr Eugene. He added that the government needs to do more for the fisherfolk to help them overcome the loss they have incurred.

Kerala Fisheries Minister, J. Mercykutty, said in March 2018 that the Centre is yet to approve a special financial package of Rs 7,340 crore for the rehabilitation and reconstruction of Ockhi-hit coastal villages. However, in July 2018, the Union government categorically stated that it is not considering Kerala's request for a special package for Cyclone Ockhi affected fisherfolk, over and above the relief that was granted as per the existing norms of disaster management. The Union Ministry was responding to a question raised by N.K. Premachandran, a parliamentarian from Kerala, in the Parliament.

People like Selin and Bernard are struggling and pinning their hopes for the future on compensation, but it doesn't seem that any help is coming.

*

Meanwhile, fishermen along the coast still believe that Ockhi was a man-made disaster. They claim that neither depression nor cyclone alerts were issued by government authorities. Irked by the 'technical snag' that occurred in alerting the fishermen, they argue that the men would have not gone fishing if they had been alerted about the danger. 'We would not have lost our brothers. One of the families in the village has lost fourteen members,' said Sebastia F., a fisherwoman. 'Who should be held responsible for this callous attitude? They failed to alert us, which is why we lost our men,' she added.

However, the director of the Indian Meteorological Department (IMD) Thiruvananthapuram, S. Sudevan, said that they had issued clear warnings on November 29 and 30 to the departments concerned. 'We said that there is a depression and it is intensifying. Our warnings also warned fishermen to not venture into the sea for the next forty-eight hours. The warning was issued periodically on [Wednesday] November 29 from 12 p.m. every three hours,' he said. He added that at 2 a.m. and 5:30 a.m. on [Thursday] November 30, his office had issued an alert saying that the depression had become deep and was expected to intensify further. 'The warnings had clear mentions about wind speed and wave heights,' Sudevan said. 'We had copied the warnings to all government departments and authorities concerned, including police stations, fisheries departments and even to radio stations.'

The IMD's November 23-30 weekly update and the 10 a.m. bulletin on November 20, both available in the public domain, clearly stated Cyclone Ockhi's strength and path. Unfortunately, the state government and its disaster management body had reportedly missed the alerts and acted too late.

On December 1, 2017, Kerala Chief Minister Pinarayi Vijayan dismissed the allegation that the government had failed to take effective steps to tackle the situation, terming it a misunderstanding about the issue. He said the state received the cyclone warning on Thursday at noon. Prior to that, there was no cyclone alert, though the general information about the weather was available. He said that as far as the state government was concerned, it could initiate emergency action only on the basis of an actual cyclone warning. He added that there was no delay on the part of the government to send relief to the victims.

An official from the State Disaster Management Authority (SDMA), which is chaired by Vijayan, also echoed the same opinion. He said that they issue a warning only when a depression turns into a cyclone. However, a former senior official at the SDMA, Keshav Mohan, said that the authority's emergency operation centre should have multi-skilled scientific experts to observe, study, analyze and advise the SDMA and the state government on time. 'Currently, the state emergency operation centre is short of experts who are capable of identifying and advising on disasters. That is why we failed to act on time. We should see this failure as a lesson and move ahead, rectifying it so that the same mistake is not repeated,' Mohan said.

Mohan's recommendations seem sound when we consider that a query filed by this author via the Right to Information (RTI) Act 2005 reveals that the Kerala government did not inspect any of their sixty-one dams before the 2018 monsoon. The Central Water Commission, replying to the RTI query, said that according to its records, two dams underwent pre-monsoon inspections in 2015, four in 2016, four in 2017 and none in 2018. When it comes to post-monsoon inspections, the CWC revealed that two were done in 2015, five in 2016, four in 2017 and four in 2018. The commission did not disclose the names of the dams inspected. Moreover, the CWC does not even have a report informing them if a dam is in critical condition or not.

Kerala has fifty-seven large dams, of which four are operated by Tamil Nadu. According to the Guidelines for Safety Inspection of Dams, 2017, regular inspections, effective instrumentation, and diligent monitoring are needed to identify potential problems and take corrective actions to reduce the risk of dam failure.

*

Meanwhile, fishermen continue to be irked by the government's cyclone alerts, alleging that it is now issuing inaccurate and unscientific alerts in the aftermath of Cyclone Ockhi. They say that these unnecessary alerts, along with the ecological damage caused due to Cyclone Ockhi, is pushing them into poverty. Jose Alwin, a fisherman in Marianad area of the Thiruvananthapuram coast says, 'After Cyclone Ockhi the frequency of these alerts is really high. Many a time, the alerts are wrong, and we just end up losing the opportunity for a catch. This is pushing us into poverty,' he said.

'Most often, we get an alert for deep depression. But the sea would be rough for only half a day—and yet, the government and others stopped the fishermen from going to sea,' says Suresh Nicholas, an official of the Marianad Fishermen Society. The numbers, fishermen say, illustrate this clearly. According to Suresh, in November 2017, the fishermen in the area were able to net fish worth Rs 2 crore in a month. In 2018, it had come down drastically. 'It ranged between Rs 60 lakh and Rs 1.2 crore per month,' he said.

Saju Antony, an activist in the coastal area, says that the government is least bothered about the livelihoods of the fishermen. 'They stop fishermen from going into the sea. But they don't provide any better support system,' Saju says. Fishermen demand that the government must provide compensation as well. 'Already, the catch is less and the support system from the government is also too low. At this juncture, the government is issuing alerts frequently, and we are stopped from going for fishing,' John Augustine, a fisherman from the Poonthura area, said.

T. Peter, General Secretary of the National Fishworkers' Forum (NFF), said that the fishermen in the coastal area are under severe financial stress. 'The number of fishing days have come down due to inaccurate alerts. And eventually, fishermen are forced to take a loan from private money lenders, which leads to many other issues,' Peter said.

According to Peter, fishermen are facing a crisis, much like the one farmers have been battling with. 'However, these fishermen have a strong will to fight the adverse conditions. That's what they have learned from fighting in killer waves. So, they don't and won't commit suicide. They are fighters. But I am worried about how long they will fight,' he said. 'If the current situation prevails, a day will come when fishermen will be in neck-deep trouble and may take drastic steps to end their lives,' Peter added.

Peter sees three main reasons for the crisis. One is financial stress due to the smaller number of fishing days, another is the lack of support from the government and the third is the implementation of pro-industrialist policies which force traditional fisherfolk to leave their homes and move to other areas where they don't know how to survive.

According to Peter, due to the lack of jobs in fishing, the younger generation is moving to other places. 'They are now working as salespersons in textile shops and for online food delivery chains. Don't they have to survive? What else can be done?' he asked. 'Due to construction activities, there is seashore erosion. And when the coast is lost, fishermen are forced to move to harbour-based fishing activities, which increases their expenses. This is affecting their earnings a lot,' he added.

\*

Having struggled through the ravages of Cyclone Ockhi, many fishermen are now boat-less daily wagers, working hard to get Rs 500 to 1000 a day to make ends meet and repay loans. Others carry the scars, mental and physical, of years of unremitting toil. Yet others have lost loved ones, lands and livelihoods to the sea. However, all of them came together, without even having to be called in many cases, to save the people of Kerala when threatened by the floods. This book is both a chronicle of their stories, and my tribute to their enduring courage.

# REFERENCES

Goswami, Samyabrata Ray. 'Mumbai gawks as train chugs overhead' in *The Telegraph* 19 February 2013. https://www.telegraphindia.com/india/mumbai-gawks-as-train-chugs-overhead-september-start-on-track-for-indias-first-monorail/cid/332693

Guidelines for Safety Inspection of Dams. Central Water Commission, June 2017.

Jacob, Meenu. '1924 Flood of Travancore: A Literary Representation' in *VISTAS: A Multidisciplinary Research Journal.*

Kerala Tourism. 'Kundala Valley Railway'. https://www.keralatourism.org/munnar/kundala-valley-railway-munnar.php

Khelkar, Pankaj K. 'Kerala floods: *India Today* digs rainfall records of 140 years in God's Own Country' in *India Today.* 22 August 2018. https://www.indiatoday.in/india/story/kerala-floods-india-today-rainfall-records-140-years-god-own-country-1320153-2018-08-22

Kuttappan, R. 'Not one dam in Kerala was inspected before monsoon, reveals RTI'. *Down To Earth.* 25 September 2018. https://www.downtoearth.org.in/news/governance/not-one-dam-in-kerala-was-inspected-before-monsoon-reveals-rti-61720

—— '"Storage, release of water in dams should be reviewed": CWC report on Kerala floods' in *The News Minute.* 12 September, 2018. https://www.thenewsminute.com/article/storage-release-water-dams-should-be-reviewed-cwc-report-kerala-floods-88242

MovingShoe. 'The great flood of 99 (1924 flood), which devastated Munnar'. http://movingshoe.com/the-great-flood-of-99-devastated-munnar/

Pillai, Manu S. *The Ivory Throne: Chronicles of the House of Travancore*. HarperCollins, 2016.

Ramaswamy, C. *Review of floods in India during the past 75 years*. Indian National Science Academy. 1985.

Roychoudhary, Adrija. 'Kerala floods: The deluge of 1924 was smaller, but impact was similar' in *The Indian Express*. 22 August 2018. https://indianexpress.com/article/research/year-1099-keralas-great-flood-of-1924-too-affected-same-areas-5317677/

Tata Central Archives. *Sands of Time*. Newsletter. http://www.tatacentralarchives.com/publications/newsletter.html

http://www.old.kerala.gov.in/keralacal_july09/pg14-15.pdf

http://thrissurpooramfestival.com/thrissur.html

http://wikimapia.org/17306917/Karinthiri

# 1

## JESUS CHRIST HAS LEFT ME ALIVE FOR A REASON...

*'I believe that Jesus Christ has left me alive to do something. Or else, why didn't he call me back when he took away my husband, elderly mother-in law and my physically challenged son?*

*'Why did he keep me alive for three days without any food?*

*'Why did he keep me alive only by drinking dirty flood water?*

*'Why didn't he let me realize that my son had also died in my hands and fallen into flood water?*

*'If he had allowed me to know or realize the fact that my son too had died, I would have done something bad.*

*'It seems, Jesus has left me alive to do something...'*

These were the words of sixty-four-year-old Annamma Varghese, a resident of Kannaada village in Chengannur, Kerala, which was badly affected during the deluge faced by the state in August 2018.

She was rescued by fishermen when she was found alone, holding the grilles of her flooded house to keep her head out of the water, and crying for help. The dead bodies of her loved ones had been lying in her bedroom for nearly twenty-four hours.

'If the boatmen had not come on August 17, I would also have died. When they arrived, it was around 4:30 p.m. I didn't realize that they had come to help me. There was around four to five feet water inside the house. The boatmen struggled to open the grille and pull me out,' she said. 'But when I was carried to the boat by the rescuers, I realized that my family's bodies were lying inside. So, I told them that I didn't want to go, leaving them behind. But the rescuers were quite good. They told me not to worry and assured me that the bodies would be brought in a following boat. So, I said yes,' explained Annamma.

When I met Annamma at her home, where she doesn't stay now because of the haunting memories, she was in a mentally disturbed state. I could see it in her manner as she recollected the traumatic memories.

I was even a bit afraid to ask her for details, worrying that it would put her into a more troubled mood. But though she had been reluctant to speak in the beginning, when she started to tell me the events of that time, it was in a continuous flow.

She was weeping as she told me about the happenings of those three bad days.

'On the afternoon itself of August 15, I could see the water levels rising in my front garden. My husband returned early from his daily walk, saying that flood waters were entering dangerously in the surrounding areas. As there had been no power supply since August 13, he had bought a few candles too,' Annamma recalled.

Annamma was living with her seventy-one-year-old husband, ninety-six-year-old mother-in-law and thirty-eight-year-old physically-challenged son. They had returned to the Kannaada house in 2010. Before that, Annamma and her family had been in Jhansi in Uttar Pradesh (UP). Her husband had worked in the Air Force and later in the Railways. Annamma, too, had been a government nurse. In 2009, her son had had a road accident and had been left crippled. Her mother-in-law was all alone in the Kannaada house. So, given all these factors, they had returned.

As her son was bed-ridden, Annamma never used to go anywhere. She had brought him to Kerala on a stretcher. 'He was conscious, but mobility was a problem. It was me who was taking care of him. It was like a hospital room here inside the house. He needed constant support,' Annamma said.

I could see that she had loved him greatly from how she spoke about her son, and that she was still struggling to overcome his loss. 'For all of us, he was everything. We all loved him a lot. Especially, my mother-in-law liked him too much. Without confirming that he had eaten, she wouldn't even have food,' Annamma said.

On the night of August 15, the rainwater had entered her house. She had had to close the back and front doors. 'In the front, we had grilles. There, I had put chairs and tables much earlier, so that the items inside the house don't get carried away outside by the water,' Annamma explained, adding that by then there was already three feet of water inside the house.

'We saw that water had started to flow over my son's cot. So, we somehow brought another bed and put it on the existing one and tried to keep him dry. And in a few hours, the candles were over. Luckily, we had a bronze lamp. My husband lit it and, with that single source of light, we all tried to hold on together while sitting on our son's cot. We hoped that the water levels would come down by early morning,' Annamma said.

But, in fact, rain worsened matters that night.

The family had only one neighbour. 'They had gone somewhere outside Kerala. So, there was no use in crying for help. But we were using the phone, desperately calling here and there for someone to help us. My husband was doing that. We both were worried about our son and mother,' Annamma said.

Her second son, who lives in Gujarat, was also desperately trying to reach out to rescuers for help over the phone from there. 'He was calling and updating us, promising that help is on the way. But nothing happened. Can't blame him—what can he do, being thousands of kilometres away from us? And did anybody expect that we will be trapped in such a deluge?' Annamma asked rhetorically.

On August 16, in the early morning, Annamma's mother-in-law told her that she wouldn't be able to hold on further. 'She just fell on to the cot where my son was lying. We understood that she had passed away,' Annamma said.

According to Annamma, the flood water was spine-chillingly cold, and the non-stop rain had worsened the situation. 'As the water had drenched the cot, we made our son stand up. But he needs support, so I held him close to my left side. The water level was rising. There was water above my waist. My legs were paining. I am also diabetic. So, it was horrible. But as I had to hold my son, I bore all the pain and prayed continuously to Jesus. What else was there to be done?' Annamma believed strongly that at least the three of them would survive.

By afternoon, her husband collapsed. 'He was diabetic. As we were not able to have food, his sugar levels went down, and he suffered palpitations. I couldn't do anything as I was holding my son. I saw his death. He fell into the water inside the same room,' Annamma said. 'The last words he said were "*Annamme... I feel tired... I don't think I can hold up any more...*"

'Although the bodies of my husband and mother-in-law were lying in front of us, my son kept asking where his father and grandma had gone. I told him that they had gone for prayers. He was not understanding what was happening,' Annamma said.

As time went by, Annamma also began getting tired. She began feeling hungry and thirsty. But as her son needed her to stand upright, she couldn't do anything. From her words, I understood that she had lost consciousness after her husband's death.

'I didn't know when I lost my son. I didn't realize when he slipped down, away from my hand. It would have happened on the night of August 16 or maybe in the afternoon. I was not aware of time. It was pitch black inside, as it had been raining non-stop, and the house is surrounded by rubber and banana trees and coffee plants. I don't know when it happened,' Annamma said.

Annamma was not able to tell me properly about what had happened after she lost her son. She removed her glasses, wiping away tears and looking at the room where everything had happened. She paused for a few seconds and then continued to talk. 'The water level kept rising. One moment I remember clearly is when I was wading through the water, and I presumed that I had gone to some other house. I couldn't even recognize my own house. But when I came to the veranda, I saw the reflection of Jesus Christ's framed picture floating on the water, from where the bronze lamp was lit. Then I realized that I am in my home itself.'

At some point after she lost her son, she came

to the veranda and stood there, holding the grilles for support. 'The water was above my waist. The household items were floating in it and hitting against me. I had suffered injuries. When I felt thirsty, I drank the dirty flood water. It seems that I was not aware of their deaths, especially the death of my son. If I had been able to understand that my son was dead, then I would also have done something bad,' Annamma said. 'I just held on to the grilles and prayed.'

Rescuers came on August 17, at around four p.m. Annamma's house is just 500 metres away from the main road. However, as the water levels were rising dangerously and threatening to cover a small bridge nearby, police officials standing guard there on boats and rooftops were not allowing boatmen to cross the area. But finally, on August 17, the rescuers risked their lives and drove their boats ahead, ignoring the warnings of the police. They crossed the flooded bridge on boats, looking for stranded people.

Annamma was rescued, and the bodies of her family were also retrieved and moved to a hospital mortuary in Chengannur. 'One of my relatives was involved in social work at the hospital and was managing the arrival of the mortal remains of those who died in the flood. He had recognized the bodies of my family. So, he took special care to find a space for them in the mortuary,' Annamma added.

During the flood, all three mortuaries in the city were full, and some were also flooded themselves. There were even reports that the bodies were floating inside one of the hospital mortuaries. Patients from that hospital had to be evacuated by boatmen and other rescuers.

Annamma was able to bury her loved ones in the family tomb in the church only ten days later, on August 27. The church, too, had suffered damage during the floods.

Annamma was not aware of her rescuers' names or other details. She had understood that the boat came from Alappuzha, a nearby coastal town famous for its backwaters, and only knew the rescuers were fishermen who had risked their lives to save people like her.

Why?

# 2

## BATMAN, SUPERMAN...FISHERMAN!

I met Saju Antony and Jack Mandalo at South Thumba shore on the Thiruvananthapuram coast, just ten days after they returned from the rescue operations in flood-submerged Chengannur. At the time, Saju was shuttling between the hospital and his home, as his father was in the intensive care unit. When Saju had gone to Chengannur to take part in the rescue operations, his father had already been unwell, but in Saju's own words, 'It didn't stop me from joining the rescue team'. He spoke about his decision in a matter-of-fact way.

'It was around six p.m. on August 16, when we first got the call from Thumba Police officials to arrange boats and head to Chengannur. I had no plans to go at all, but when Jack told me to join in, I handed over my motorcycle to a friend and took the lead in getting it all arranged,' Saju said. He had a feeling that his family wouldn't agree to his going for rescue work, so he decided not to ask for their permission. 'I was aware that my family will panic if I tell them that I am going to get involved in flood rescue operations. I knew that if I ask for permission, they would stop me,' he said. 'So I planned it well. I told my friend not to drop my bike off at home until the next day, and not tell them anything.'

Jack and Saju both belong to the fisherfolk community in Thumba. Although Saju is involved in coordination for the welfare of fishermen, it's Jack who has been a regular sea-goer since the time they both returned from the Gulf. When I met them, Saju was enthusiastic, easily excited and talkative. Jack was more silent but also more easy-going. He seemed to think that their experiences were not such a big deal. 'We have braved twelve-foot-high pounding waves in the sea. I have manned boats while in a cyclone. So why will these floods frighten us?' he asked.

\*

'On television and through social media we'd been seeing the floodwaters rising in Aluva [a town near Ernakulam, the commercial capital of Kerala]. So, we were aware of the situation, and decided that wasting even a minute would endanger the lives of hundreds,' Saju explained. Saju and Jack arranged for eighteen boats from the South Thumba area, calling enough fishermen that each boat was manned by five people. They also arranged for small lorries to transport the boats via road to Chengannur. 'By late night on August 16, we had left our village. Our aim was to reach Chengannur as early as possible,' Saju recalled.

While they talk about the preparations they had made, I can feel the energy still running through them, the enthusiasm and anxiety they had undergone during those three days of rescue operations. Jack recalled, 'When the police called and told me that we must go to Chengannur, I didn't even think twice. I simply rushed to South Thumba junction, without even a plastic carry bag.' It is very common for Keralites, especially for those from villages or coastal areas, to carry a change of clothes and some basic toiletries like toothpaste and brush, bath soap and a small cloth towel, in a plastic bag, usually from a local textile shop. With that bag, they feel equipped to travel anywhere in India.

Jack described the scene. 'While some men had bags, most of them didn't. Many presumed that they would return in one day. As Saju joined us at the last minute, he also didn't have anything.'

Since the police had called them at such short notice, many of them didn't even have any money either. 'Actually, we didn't think of money. We just got on to the lorries. It was raining heavily too,' Saju said.

*

On August 17 at around 10:30 a.m., Saju, Jack and their convoy of lorries reached Pandalam, the town where Lord Ayyappa is believed to have been brought up. From there, they were told to head to Aranmula in Chengannur. Heavy rains had started on August 13, worsening day by day, and had submerged Chengannur totally by the time Saju and Jack arrived. 'When we reached Aranmula, we couldn't understand which is the road and which is the river,' Jack said.

Late on the night of August 14, the Pamba River had started to overflow. The shutters of the Kochupampa and Anathode-Kakki dams, which provide water to the Sabarigiri Hydroelectric Plant in Pathanamthitta district had been opened due to rising water levels, to avoid a dam breach. According to the data released by the State Disaster Management Authority, 85,300 litres of water was being released every second from

Kakki-Anathode dam, and 47,000 litres per second from Pampa Dam at four p.m. on August 14.

The shutters of both dams were raised at night. By ten p.m., 4.68 lakh litres of water had started gushing out of both dams. By one a.m. on August 15, this rose to 6.5 lakh litres per second and, by six a.m., to 9.39 lakh litres per second.

While people in Chengannur were glued to their television sets, watching the flood in Aluva and Ernakulam, they were taken by surprise when the flood waters started to enter their own homes.

*

'We realized that the situation was worse than we'd expected,' Jack explained. 'People were panicking badly. While some were crying, others ran here and there. Everybody had only one request for us: get the boats unloaded as soon as possible and rescue their dear ones marooned in their houses.'

As Saju and Jack were unfamiliar with the area, the social workers trying to organize flood rescues had arranged for a local person to go on the boat with them as a guide through lanes that were flooded with over six feet of rushing water.

'Even though people were literally dragging us to

help them in reaching their stranded relatives, we were told that we have to head to a nearby hospital which was completely flooded,' Jack remembered. 'When we reached the hospital, the water was so high that the only way to reach the stranded people was for us to push the boat into the building!'

Jack and Saju had to rescue several people, including a seventy-year-old differently-abled man and a young woman with her nine-day-old baby girl, from the flooded hospital. Many of them had been admitted while suffering from the flu and were now exposed to the rain and dirty water.

'There were sixteen people to be rescued from the hospital. Additionally, we had to carry an aged man who needed an oxygen cylinder. So, we decided to split them into two groups,' Jack said. In the first group, Saju and Jack took the mother, baby and a few others. The aged man on oxygen support was taken in the second trip, after shifting the first group to a shelter nearby.

'Rescuing the mother and baby was not much of a hassle. But moving the old man and his oxygen cylinder was a tricky one. We had to take care of the boat, the other people on board and move the man and his oxygen support without hurting him. It was raining heavily throughout. But there were no options other than taking the risk,' Jack said.

Driving the boat back to the shelter was also riskier on this trip, according to them. 'There were strong undercurrents in many places. The oxygen cylinder had to be kept in a vertical position. It was shaking the boat a lot. However, our boat driver, Anto Eliaz, did a commendable job. He is a regular sea-goer and we had confidence with him,' Jack said.

Jack, Saju and his team were involved in rescue operations till late in the evening on that day. 'We didn't have any mobile phones or special lamps. The only aid we had was the local guide who knew the area well. We would hear people shouting for help when they heard our engine,' Saju said.

On the first day itself, they were able to rescue around 600 people.

*

After the long day, Saju and Jack took shelter in a temple auditorium provided by the local authorities.

'We didn't even have a change of dress. We slept in the same drenched clothes. It was a flood relief camp. Everyone was in the same situation. We got some of the food being distributed to all. We didn't ask for anything extra. I just found a corner and tried to catch some sleep,' Jack said.

'Rescuing so many people on the first day itself had boosted our confidence and gave us a great feeling,' chimed in Saju.

*

On the next day, August 18, Saju, Jack and his team left the shelter at around six a.m. 'We didn't wait for breakfast. When we looked out of the shelter, we found that the flood water had risen. There had been heavy rain during the night, so we were expecting this,' Jack said.

Although the police, flood relief organizers and the government wanted fishermen to come to the flooded area with their boats, neither the fishermen nor the rescued people were given lifejackets. 'So, we had to be extra cautious,' Saju explained. 'Many of the people had not even seen a fishing boat before. It was a herculean task to rescue them. The bruises we suffered while driving the boat, climbing walls and removing steel gates during the rescue operations have not healed,' he said.

Jack added that they were still taking medicines to avoid skin diseases they could have contracted while swimming in overflowing sewage and flood water. 'Even now, each of us can sense that dirty smell. I still feel that even the new t-shirt I'm wearing now is wet and muddy.'

'But we are happy. We were able to save at least a thousand people from marooned and submerged houses,' Saju added. On the second day, Saju and Jack were able to rescue about 400 people more.

*

'On that day, as the flood waters were higher, we were facing problems. Our boat would keep hitting gates and walls covered by water, sometimes even the roofs of small shops. With every hit, not only was our boat getting damaged, but we were also worrying about the rescued people on board. The majority of them had no experience in boats, and we had to teach them how to balance themselves so that the boat wouldn't tip over,' Jack said.

'While occasionally we had children on board, most of the time it was old people. Aged parents, whose children are working abroad to earn...' he remembered. The Kerala Migration Study 2018 reveals that Chengannur is one of the areas of the state where more than 20 per cent of the population are living abroad. Most of the bungalows in Chengannur are lived in by senior citizens, as their grown-up children generally work in the Middle East, Europe and the United States.

Jack described some of the challenges of flood rescue in this situation: 'The majority of the people we were trying to rescue were heavily built, aged or even bedridden. So, getting them on board the boat was quite a task.'

Saju also recollected his memories of that day. 'As the water level was high, and people were not used to sitting in a boat, one elderly person fell inside the boat while we were trying to bring him on board. This shook the boat badly, and we realized that we wouldn't be able to move forward with that many people on board and such a badly shaken boat. Two of our friends got down and swam in that dirty water while pushing the boat forward!'

He describes another incident during the same day, when again his team had to take huge risks to bring stranded people to safety. 'When we reached a house, we saw that there was only an elderly couple, probably in their late seventies. They had taken shelter on the second floor. The water was around twelve feet high by then.'

According to Jack and Saju, when they tried to enter the compound of the house to dock the boat at the second floor, it hit the huge gate. 'When the boat hit the gate, we thought we all will fall out. After we managed to save ourselves, we realized that the boat was stuck on the gate and we couldn't move forward. One of our friends jumped from the boat. He took a deep dive, and somehow, he managed to push the boat upwards,' Jack said. 'The water was dirty but it didn't stop him.' The man then pushed the boat towards the second floor of the building.

The team tied the boat to the railings on the second floor to hold it in a stable position, while Jack climbed on to the second floor. He tied the elderly woman to him with a rope. Saju, meanwhile, had knotted another rope onto the railing.

'We held one end of the rope firmly inside the boat. We are good at braving the water and waves and driving the boat, but this kind of rescue operation was new to us. We didn't have any backup. If something had gone wrong and Jack and the old lady had fallen into the water, then it would have been a tragedy,' Saju said soberly. 'Jack would have managed to save himself, if he'd been alone. But think of the elderly couple. They were both heavily built and aged too.

They wouldn't have had any experience in swimming either. Often, people who don't know how to swim will pull down the rescuing person as well, in a bid to save themselves,' he explained. 'So, we were extra cautious.

'We had to make sure that we held the rope steady and pulled taut while Jack slid down it with the old lady. At the same time, we had to make sure that they landed properly inside the boat without tipping it over,' Saju explained.

According to Jack, he was confident in his ability to rescue the elderly couple safely, but it was difficult for him to convince the others—and the two old and scared people—that he could do it.

'Despite everything, it took around thirty minutes for me to convince them that I could take them down to the boat safely. Somehow, I managed to do so. I first tied the lady to me and slowly slipped down, holding the rope tightly. She was quite heavy. I could see Saju and my friends struggling while holding the other end of the rope. They gave me the signal, and with a tight grip on the rope, we slid down to the boat,' Jack said. 'When the old lady touched the boat, I could see the relief on her face. She was crying.'

Saju and the others, too, had the same feeling.

'Deep in our hearts, we were not that confident about Jack being able to pull off such a text-book landing. However, it happened,' Saju said.

And, in the next attempt, Jack brought down the elderly man as well.

*

Characteristically, Jack didn't want to dwell on his bravery during this rescue. He began telling me about an incident he couldn't forget, that occurred while he was rescuing a family.

'There were seven people in that two-storey building. They had been stranded without food or even drinking water for two days. They were all in bad shape, and one elderly diabetic person was in an acute condition. We rescued all of them, one by one, with our limited resources, mainly using ropes and our own bodily strength. When everyone was on board, one of the young girls became very agitated, telling us again and again that "Pinky is stuck inside". We couldn't understand. We thought Pinky must be a little girl, so, we asked her to tell us where she is. The girl replied that Pinky was on the left room of the second floor.

'I had started climbing to the second floor from the boat with a rope, when she said that Pinky was their

Pomeranian dog. I was shocked. I even thought about just turning and climbing back down to the boat. But when I saw that girl's face, and her determination that she won't leave without their pet, I decided to go ahead. When I reached the room, I saw the dog, took it in my arms and came back to the boat,' Jack finished.

According to Saju and Jack, many people had left their expensive pets locked in cages. 'Many seemed to be dead. The owners could have unchained them. They would have at least tried to escape,' Saju said.

Saju had a happier memory from the same day. 'While we were bringing back rescued people to the shelter, the rain suddenly became very strong. The flood waters were continuing to rise. The boat was shaking and every few minutes we would hit against the rooftops of submerged one-storey buildings. The people with us were terrified, because they thought they will fall out of the boat. Many were crying and a few started to pray. At that point, there was a Christian, a Muslim and a Hindu in the boat. All three started to pray together. I heard Christian, Muslim and Hindu prayers at the same time in our boat!'

But the flood rescue had taken its toll on him as well. He remembered that, on the first day itself, while they were crossing a certain lane, they could hear a cry for help. But they failed to pinpoint the location and couldn't reach out to help the stranded person. 'When we left Chengannur on the night of August 18, it was haunting me. I can still hear that cry for help; it keeps haunting me. Maybe somebody else rescued them... We couldn't do anything for them. I can't forget that cry still,' Saju said.

\*

On August 18, Saju and his team ended their rescue operations by five p.m. and started their return journey. Meanwhile, traditional and new media, both offline and online, had already started to report the heroic acts of these fishermen. But Saju and the others who were involved in the operation were not at all aware of this.

'While returning late at night, we stopped at a small hotel to have food, some sixty kilometres away from the flood-hit area. There were about fifteen of us. While serving the food, the hotel manager asked us whether we were the fishermen who had been involved in the rescue operations. We said yes. I could see love and happiness in his eyes. He was very polite while speaking to us, and sounded quite grateful. He said that if we had not jumped to the rescue, the death toll would have gone up,' Saju remembered, adding that the hotel manager refused to take money for the food they ate. 'He said "You people risked your lives and saved people. Let me at least do this."

'It was only then that we got any idea that we were being revered as the saviours of Kerala. He even showed as a poster on his phone, which read "If Hollywood has Superman and Batman, Kerala has Fishermen!"' Saju laughed.

Saju, Jack and their team had rescued nearly 1,200 stranded people in Chengannur in two days. 'We felt happy. We did something which will not be forgotten by people in their lifetimes,' they said.

# 3

## THEY DIDN'T EVEN REALIZE THE EFFORT WE WERE MAKING

'Can people be self-centred, even when they are in trouble? I am not. Others I know are not. These people are richer and better educated than us, but they were selfish and greedy. Even when they were neck-deep in trouble, they were selfish. It was painful to learn that. They even didn't realize the effort we were making...'

This was the issue troubling Joseph Francis who travelled some 200 kilometres from Thiruvananthapuram, to Venmani village in flood-hit Chengannur, to rescue stranded people. But, instead of recounting his own exploits, he kept coming back to this question again and again during his conversation with me.

Joseph, a father of four, was not worried about risking his life in Chengannur. 'When the priest in the church sought our help, I boarded the truck carrying our boat in Poonthura,' he told me, describing the place as a coastal village in Thiruvananthapuram district. 'Before leaving, I made the decision that I would save at least five lives. With God's grace, we were able to save around 470 lives in two days. We jumped into flood waters with empty stomachs. We carried people on our shoulders. We ignored our injuries. We were not afraid of snakes and scorpions... When we saw how self-centred people can be, we were disappointed. But we didn't give up.'

Joseph and three fishermen friends started their journey to Chengannur late at night on August 16. While they were approaching the flood-hit area, they saw many small trucks returning, loaded with boats. They were turning back because of the heavy current from the water flooding the roads.

'Our driver also became worried, but I persuaded him to take the risk,' Joseph said. 'I thought that we have travelled for over a hundred kilometres and made so many arrangements to get here... How can we return without doing anything? "Let's give it a try," I told him. He was still a bit reluctant, but when I told him that we have come to save lives, he agreed. He knew we had to do that at any cost.

'We continued to drive slowly through the rising water. At one point, he was losing control of the truck. It was pushed all the way to the left side of the road by the force of the water. But our driver was not ready to give up. He pressed the gas, upped the gear and managed to move the vehicle. Somehow, we managed to cross that flooded road.

'When we reached Venmani, we got a local person to guide us. With him on board, we started the rescue operations. The area was like an ocean. We could only see some roofs of half-flooded houses, with large gaps where other buildings were fully submerged. The flood waters spread in every direction. We would cross a section with faster current, and the local guide would tell us that we are driving down a road or crossing a stream. There was no way for us to tell where we were.'

But Joseph and his friends were not at all afraid of the situation. Joseph is a Cyclone Ockhi survivor. On November 29, 2017, he and his four friends were thrown into the water, after their boat broke some 30 nautical miles out at sea from the Poonthura shore. For three continuous days, they floated in the sea without food or water, braving huge waves and heavy rains from the cyclone.

'Our boat broke when it was hit by a heavy wave. We lost everything. However, we were lucky enough to catch hold of a bamboo stick from the broken boat. We all tied one hand to the stick, so that we wouldn't lose track of each other when the waves threw us up and down,' Joseph recalled. 'We were all in bad shape. We thought that we wouldn't survive. The spine-chillingly cold water was painful, and our legs screamed with pain from our continuous efforts to remain afloat,' he recounted the struggle. 'Three days...it was raining like hell. It was dark. We were all so frightened.'

On the third day, Joseph saw a fishing boat. 'We used all our energy for shouting to get their attention. And when they saw us, we literally begged them to save us. They neared the bamboo stick and pulled us from the water. But by then, the fourth person with us had died. We couldn't even find his body. He was lost.'

The fishing boat was from Colachel, a fishing port on the southern tip of Tamil Nadu. They took Joseph and his two friends back there. After reaching dry land, they called their homes. 'At my home, they thought that I had died. They had lost all hope and were waiting only for my body. They had even put garlands on my picture. When I called them on the

phone, it took a few minutes for them to accept that
I am alive,' he said.

Cyclone Ockhi claimed 174 lives. Apart from the
official death toll, 261 people had gone missing and
were never found. Joseph's friend who died in the
water was brought back for burial in the village. 'We
were updated by the authorities about his mortal
remains after ten days. He had been found on the
northern coast of Kerala,' Joseph said.

'I have seen death in front of me. I have seen rough
seas. Monster waves have thrown us up and down
for three days. I have experienced how, if we stand
together, we can survive. So, I was not afraid of the
flood or of losing my life. That's why I volunteered to
join the rescue operations in Chengannur,' he explained
to me. 'But a few people disappointed me a lot... Still,
I can't help feeling pity for them...'

*

Joseph was talking about an incident that occurred
during the flood rescue operations. Some of the people
that he and his friends had rescued refused to admit
other stranded people on to the boat.

'It happened on the second day. We had around
fifteen people on the boat, apart from the three of us.

The water level was rising. The boat was a bit shaky too, as the people didn't know how to sit on a boat to keep it steady. We were slowly making our way towards the shelter camp, when we heard a cry for help,' he remembered.

'We took a detour and saw that the cry we'd heard came from a pregnant woman and two small children, standing on the roof terrace of a house. Drenched in rain and without any food, they were in a terrible situation. I realized that she was suffering and in pain. The children, too, were crying, seeing their mother's suffering. They immediately began begging us to take them to shelter. We started towards them, to take them on board. But, to our complete shock, some of the people on the boat refused to accommodate them!

'We were all Christians and Muslims on the boat, and it was clear that the stranded family were Hindus. But those who were on the boat had been pulled out from the flood water by myself and my friends risking our lives. We had carried them on our shoulders. Some were even close to death, exposed to the elements without food or shelter for so long. It was these people who were forcing us not to take the pregnant woman and children on board,' Joseph said, the bewilderment still plain in his voice even after several months.

'I was mentally stuck for a few moments when I heard them saying that we should leave the pregnant woman and children there and move ahead. When I came back to my senses, I shouted at them. I told them, "I came to rescue life. I will do that any cost. Even if I die, I will take you all, including the pregnant woman and children, safe to the shelter. Without them, I am not going to drive the boat."'

Joseph's friends also agreed with him. 'Ignoring the resistance from the people on board, we docked the boat near the house. We used ropes to climb on to the roof. First, we carried the children to the boat and then the pregnant lady,' Joseph said. 'She was quite heavy, and sometimes crying out in pain too. I could see that she was nearing her delivery date, and I was afraid that it was risky to carry her, but there was no other way to bring her down to the boat. I literally had to carry her in my arms. My friends helped me when I was stepping back into the boat. One of them got into the water and held the boat steady so that it wouldn't lurch about when I stepped into it. Somehow, we managed to get her on the boat.

'When they were safely on the boat, we gave them biscuits and drinking water. I could see how hungry they were,' Joseph said. 'On the way back, the woman told us they'd been literally starving for the last two days. She said that she could only manage to get some rice soup for her children. She was so afraid that they would all die.'

After Joseph finished narrating the story of the pregnant woman and her children, he was silent for a while. Then he asked me why people behave like the ones in the boat. 'They have enough money and live in two-storey houses. But it seems they have forgotten how to be compassionate to fellow human beings,' he said.

*

Financially, Joseph has been struggling, as he lost his boat in Ockhi. 'It was bought on loan. Still, the loan is pending. Now, these days I'm going as a daily wager. Sometimes, I get Rs 500 and sometimes Rs 1,000 per day. But there is no guarantee of getting a job daily. So, it's quite difficult to survive,' he said.

He has three sons and a daughter. One son, who is blind, is studying in a school in Varkala, about 50 kilometres away from his home. 'His brother is also in the same school, helping him. The other two study here, in my village,' he explained. 'Here, we are poor. But we don't ditch each other. We don't say no to anybody. Why do rich people do that? Why are they like that? I can't still get rid of that bad experience…'

I just smiled. I couldn't answer. I wanted to say that rich people are less compassionate. However, I was not sure whether I was right. Can we generalize that all rich people are less compassionate and more greedy? I am not sure. So, I didn't say anything. Joseph shook my hand and walked away.

# 4

## COASTAL WARRIORS

Neither Johny Chekkitta nor his friends owned a fishing boat. But when Johny received a call on August 16 from a friend in Chengannur, seeking help for flood rescue, he didn't think twice. They hired a boat from a friend, arranged for a small pick-up jeep, and drove to Chengannur, which is 150 kilometres from their fishing hamlet on the coast of Thiruvananthapuram.

'We have seen the rough seas. We have braved high tides. Even if we are thrown into the sea for four days, we can survive. So, we were confident that we can do something in the flood-hit area. We were sure that we would be able to save lives, and not drown in the flood waters. That confidence was the only thing we had, but it helped us in saving lives,' said Johny, who captained a seven-member team during the flood rescue operations. The team comprised Johny and his friends, John Mathew, Silvadasan Antony, Aneesh Pathrose, Rateesh Peter, Jineesh Jerome and Vipin Andrews.

On the morning of August 17, when Johny's team reached Chengannur, they were told to register at a government office in order to get involved in the rescue operations. While waiting to do so, they got an emergency call saying that about a hundred people were waiting to be rescued, and that they were in a dangerous situation. As the telephone network was feeble, the coordinators on the ground were sending recorded messages, with the route and location. 'That was enough for us,' Johny told me. 'Hearing the message, we skipped the registration and headed directly into rescue work. We would replay the recorded message and drive our boat according to the directions given on it.'

Aneesh, who navigated the boat, said that it was quite risky. Aneesh is a regular sea-goer, but he found steering through the flood-hit area terrifying. 'It's not like the sea,' he explained. 'The houses were in alleys, and the flood water was flowing full steam, with a heavy current. If we wanted to take a left into an alley, we needed the whole team to exert their full strength about 10 metres before reaching the mouth of the alleyway, in order to slide the boat into it. Very often, we would hit against walls and other objects. I still can't believe how we managed to reach so many places, where even the Indian Navy boats couldn't enter.'

Rateesh added, 'Even if we managed to reach close to a house, we weren't able to dock the boat, because of the barbed wire fences, so we used to get down and swim with ropes tied to the boat. Once, one us fell into a well. Who knows what was under the water there. Everywhere you looked, there was mud-coloured water. But somehow, we managed to save many lives. That's enough,' he concluded.

Johny took up the thread of the story. 'On the first day of rescue operations, we were shuttling between marooned houses and a shelter camp. Every time we reached the shelter camp to drop off the rescued people, we saw an elderly man crying and pleading for help. He was begging the boats ahead of us to rescue some small children and old people who had taken shelter on the terrace of a building. They had been without food for the last two days. The boats ahead of us had already got calls to rescue other people, so they were not able to consider his plea. But we decided to help him. We told him to come on board and show us the way. As the flood water had made the entire area like an ocean, it didn't take us much time to reach the house.

'What we saw there is still a shocking memory. Three small children, one toddler, an elderly man and woman, and a few other people, were huddled together on top of a terrace, drenched in rain. The old man had given his shirt to cover the toddler and was shivering in the cold. They hadn't eaten for two days and their faces were completely hopeless.

'We didn't delay any more. My friends jumped into the flood water and swam towards the building. They threw a rope up to the terrace and knotted it. Then, they climbed up and brought the three children down in one go. After that, the old woman was brought down safely,' Johny remembered. 'If the old man hadn't been with us as a guide, we would never have reached the spot and rescued them. And if we hadn't gone there, or if we'd even delayed our attempt, they would have died. They were in that dire a situation.'

*

On the morning of August 18, these daring fishermen got a call from a police officer. Twenty-seven children were marooned in an orphanage, without food and drinking water. Attempts to air-lift them out had failed, and another team of fishermen had already unsuccessfully tried to rescue them on the previous day. The water had receded a bit since then, so Johny's team resolved to rescue the children at any cost. Shabu, a policeman from Chengannur station who was accompanying the team, strengthened their resolve by telling them that it would be too late if the rescue was not carried out that day itself. Despite their best intentions, when the team set out towards the orphanage, they had to stop and rescue several others and then return to drop them off to safety, as they could not ignore the pleas of starved victims crying for help.

The orphanage was in a by-lane that only a person with local knowledge could navigate. Jomon, a bus conductor from the area, travelled with the team to guide them as they battled the strong currents.

'When we reached the house, we tied our boat to a pillar, as the water was some eight feet high and we couldn't reach any closer to the doors. We realized that the children wouldn't be able to board the boat on their own; they were all on the upper floors and none of them could swim. So, other than one person manning the engine, the rest of us all jumped into the water. We couldn't see anything in that fast-flowing muddy water; there could have been snakes or sharp objects, but we were ready to carry the children in our arms and on our backs.

'We tied our rope to the doors and staircase railings, as we made our way up to where the children were all huddled together. Then, one by one, we picked up each child and passed him or her along the rope, on to another teammate, who was treading water or holding on to the rope, making a human chain. This way, within an hour, we were able to evacuate all twenty-seven children onto the boat.

'But by the time we rescued all of them, the water level was beginning to rise again, and we could feel the heavy undercurrent in the water. We were scared that with so many people in the boat—twenty-seven children and seven adults—that it might overturn in the erratic current. At times we felt that we wouldn't be able to control the boat and steer it back to the shelter at all. Somehow, despite the water levels and the current, we managed to reach the vicinity of the shelter.

'Once there, we realized that we wouldn't be able to drive the boat into the shelter, so we jumped into the water and tied ourselves to the boat. We again made a human chain and passed the children one by one to the people from the shelter, who took them into the first dry space they had seen in days.

'Getting the children out of the flooded house and then handing them over to the shelter was the riskiest thing we did,' said Johny.

After the rescue of the orphans, the next day, Saji Cherian, Chengannur's MLA, joined these seven fishermen in rescue operations. 'While returning from the orphanage after rescuing the children and the warden, the team were greeted by residents with their hands cupped in prayer.'

*

After working nearly twenty hours a day on the rescue operations, the fishermen used to snatch a few hours of sleep and shelter in a lodge near a temple. They used to eat the food given there as well. But for most of their time in Chengannur, they were shuttling non-stop with boatloads of frightened, hurt and hungry people who had been stranded for days in the flood water. Sometimes they had to make hard decisions.

'We got a call that there is a pregnant woman waiting for help and we rushed there,' recounted Silvadasan Antony. 'We rescued that woman and several other people. While returning, we got another call that nearby there is another pregnant woman in a bad condition. But we already had two dozen rescued people on our boat and there was simply no room. But none of us felt that we could ignore the call or, given the condition of the woman, delay her rescue to another trip. So, Vipin and Jineesh got down from the boat and swam to a safe place. That way, we got room to accommodate the pregnant woman and bring everybody to the shelter.'

From the morning of August 17 till the night of August 20, the team saved 800 stranded people, including pregnant women, toddlers, the twenty-seven orphans, and innumerable aged, infirm or bedridden people from marooned houses in Pandanad, the worst flood-hit area in Chengannur.

'Even though the Central Industrial Security Force, Border Security Force, Indian Navy, Air Force and National Disaster Response Force had beefed up their rescue operations, we realized that we, too, have a vital role to play,' Vipin Andrews said.

The Kerala government had announced an award of Rs 3,000 for the fishermen who were involved in the rescue operations, but these seven fishermen had refused to take it. 'We did it all to save lives. So, we don't want the reward. We have asked the authorities to deposit that money in the Chief Minister's Disaster Relief Fund,' John Mathew said.

*

Ironically, as Johny and his team had failed to register with the government on the first day, they were ignored during the official recognitions for flood rescue work. The Kerala government, churches and many social organizations had organized events to thank the fishermen and recognize their efforts in saving lives, but Johny and his team were ignored in government programmes. Expressing solidarity with Johny, Saju Antony and his team also refused to accept recognitions from the government as long as Johny and his team were excluded from the list.

Meanwhile, Johny and his team are planning to buy the boat which they used to save 800 people, and then put it up for auction. 'We are planning to offer the proceeds to the Chief Minister's Relief Fund,' Johny said.

# 5

## SOCIAL MEDIA RESCUES

Stephin Tom and his friends had just returned from the day's work, when they met me at the Thumba Church late in the evening. It was drizzling, so we decided to sit under a tent built in front of the church to chat.

Stephin is from the fishermen community, but he works as a headloader in an industrial area nearby. Survival is a daily hassle for Stephin and his friends, but they were keen to travel to Chengannur to join the rescue operations, after seeing the flood situation on TV.

Stephin's friend, Roy Rose Joseph, went live on Facebook stating that they had a boat ready in Thiruvananthapuram and were willing to join the rescue operations.

'Within seconds, after we went live on FB, we got a

call,' Roy said. The caller was in Thiruvananthapuram, dropping somebody off at the airport. While there, he got a call from his friend in the Gulf, telling him that their parents were stuck in Chengannur. 'Our FB live caught his attention and he called us, saying that his friend's family is marooned. He pleaded with us to rescue them. We immediately said yes and started our truck,' Roy explained.

'Some thirty of our friends loaded the boat on the truck and we started the journey, picking up the caller from a common meeting point in Thiruvananthapuram. That's how we joined the rescue operations,' Stephin said.

Stephin was accompanied by his friends Roy Rose Joseph, Binu Jerome, Vijo Varghese, Bijo Varghese, Sibi, Jackson and a few others.

'Among the friends, seventeen-year-old Vijo was a crazy guy. He could jump into flood water, risking his life with a smile. Once, when we couldn't enter a house with our boat as its door was stuck with mud, he dived into the water and moved the mud with his hands. I, too, did the same. Taking dives again and again, in one hour, we were able to push open the door and enter the house, where aged people were stranded,' Roy said.

They were able to rescue some 300 people during the two-day operations.

*

Social media was a great help during the Kerala floods. With traditional phone networks disrupted due to the weather, many flood victims started uploading videos to Facebook and Twitter to ask for help. Keralites around the world, who had stranded friends and relatives also uploaded videos requesting rescue teams to act quickly and save their lives. Hashtags like #KeralaFloods and #KeralaFloodRelief became popular on the Internet.

Messaging platforms like WhatsApp were filled with information, emergency numbers and details about those who were stranded. Twitter, Facebook, and particularly WhatsApp, became useful in disseminating emergency contacts, SOS messages and the immediate locations of those stuck in the calamity. This helped rescue teams reach people who needed help. Networks were full of important helpline numbers and safe locations for those not in immediate need of rescue, but who still needed help.

The authorities were also using the Internet and social media to assist those in need. The Kerala

State Disaster Management Authority put up mobile numbers asking people to send their locations via WhatsApp. The state government used Google Maps to create the option of letting citizens upload their locations, simplifying the process of targeting rescue operations and sending rescuers where help was needed. Keralarescue.in, another initiative by the state government, allowed people to seek or offer relief. By visiting the website, one could request for help, donate, find a relief centre, get important contact information, and/or volunteer services.

Some of the district collectors were live-transmitting their coordination of rescue operations, updating the flood situation in their jurisdiction, appealing for relief materials and communicating with flood rescue and relief volunteers.

Along with the state government, common people, too, were relying on digital solutions to help the flood-hit state. A group of freelancers across Twitter designed a platform on Google Maps that compiles and provides verified locations for shelter, rescue, food and water, volunteers, relief collection, transportation, medicines and more across Kerala. According to news reports during the flood, the government administration offered full support for the initiative, with chief secretary Tom Jose and IT secretary M. Sivasankar extending all possible coordination for the team, which also liaised with the Chief Minister's IT contact person, Arun Balachandran, who became one of the main links with the government for the volunteering group.

Organizations including Bhoomika Trust, Amritha Institute, Infosys, and other companies like OrisysIndia, Phykon and Sysfore, helped the group establish call centres in Thiruvananthapuram, Kochi and Kozhikode, as well as at places outside the state, like Bengaluru and Chennai. In a span of five days during the flood, the call centres handled over 30,000 phone calls effectively.

*

When Johny uploaded the video of the orphanage rescue operation on Facebook, it was viewed 1.5 million times, shared 48,000 times, and had 10,000 comments congratulating the team, within two days.

Even while involved in rescue work, the seven men were recording and transmitting the flood operations live on Facebook, taking turns in order to save the battery lives of their phones. According to them, this turned out to be great idea, and helped many people.

Johny had given his phone number on his Facebook account, and that allowed people to reach out to them in real time during the rescue work.

Silvadasan Antony gave an example. 'On August 20, while Johny was going live on FB covering the rescue operations, we got a call from a woman named Leena Susan Mathew in the United States! She said that we'd just crossed the house where her parents were stranded. We turned the boat and rescued her parents.'

Thanking Johny, Leena posted on her Facebook that they were true heroes. She wrote:

> Glory to God for keeping my parents safe at home during disaster. My heartfelt thanks to Johny Chekkitta (Good Samaritan) and his Costal Warriors [sic] (fishermen team) for rescuing my parents from our house. Last night God bought you and MLA Saji to Medapadi and Pandnad [sic] with live videos. They are without water or food for past days. Taking them to Century Hospital since mom is weak. Thank you Jesus for answering everyone's prayer and keeping my parents safe.

'Leena has assured me that she will come and meet us,' Johny added.

*

Social media also helped Kerala get financial and humanitarian assistance from people across India and the globe. Celebrities, influencers and people in authority were able to raise awareness about the floods and urge people to donate cash and other necessary items. This was almost as important as the actual rescue operations, as Roy and his friends found out after the first day, when they were getting exhausted and feeling weak due to lack of food.

'Many of the rescued people had not been able to get food, or had been surviving on limited food, since the beginning of the rains. So, by the time we rescued them, they were already tired. And the shelter camps did not have enough to meet the demand,' Stephin said. 'We were also not able to get food, medicine and other essentials for survival. So, on the first night itself, we started sending messages to friends in our village to collect essential items and bring them as soon as possible.'

Their friends in Thiruvananthapuram started to collect relief materials late on the first night itself. By morning, they had managed to collect useful items worth Rs 1,50,000. They loaded a truck and reached Chengannur by afternoon itself.

But there was a challenge waiting for them. They

were not able to take their truck to the shelters where the items were needed. They had to walk along the rail tracks for kilometres in the rain to bring the materials to the needy people in the shelter. 'They had to repeat the task again and again. There were some ten friends who had come along with the load. They all carried one or two boxes on their shoulders and walked the five to seven kilometres on the rail tracks to the shelter camps,' Stephin said.

Stephin said the rescue team felt happy only when they saw their friends. 'It was like we were also victims of the flood. As we were not getting proper food or any dry clothes to change into, we also felt that we were one of the stranded people left helpless by the flood,' he said. 'When we saw the food and clothes our friends had brought, we were quite happy and excited. And when we saw the people in shelters looking at the packages our friends had brought for them, then we realized how important it was to bring them relief materials, now that they were in a safe place,' he said.

After two days, with much satisfaction and happiness, Stephin and his friends returned to Thiruvananthapuram.

# 6

## A WAY OF LIFE, WASHED AWAY

Shabi Panipicha, a thirty-nine-year-old fisherman from Vettucaud on the Thiruvananthapuram coast, has been suffering from neck arthritis since 2015. According to his medical advisors, he is not supposed to be in the cold for a long time or carry heavy weights, especially on his shoulders. But he doesn't listen to his medics very much, and they can't stop him either.

'Jesus will take care of me,' shrugged Shabi, who jumped into action to save lives in flood-hit Chengannur. He and his friends rescued around 400 people over two-and-a-half days in Pandanad village, which was totally under water. 'I was on a mission to save lives. So, I know that Jesus will save mine.'

Like many of the fishermen involved in flood rescue operations, Shabi doesn't own a boat. Several of them had lost their boats during Cyclone Ockhi in 2017.

Like Shabi, many of them work for other boat owners on daily wages, netting between Rs 500 to Rs 3,000 per day, depending on the catch. Without a boat, it's quite hard for them to make ends meet, as the daily wage jobs are irregular. Many factors, ranging from climate change to weather conditions to international trawling norms, affect the availability of fishing jobs on a daily basis and there are sometimes gaps as long as five days between working stints.

'It's quite difficult here. We are always struck by poverty. But the fighting spirit in us makes us move ahead. We don't believe in kneeling down. We are fighters,' Shabi explained proudly when I asked him about his life. 'That's the same spirit we took to Chengannur.'

When he saw on the news that hundreds were in danger in Chengannur, Shabi had to first ask his employer to loan him a boat. The moment his employer was convinced, Shabi and two friends loaded it onto a truck and headed off.

'When we reached Pandanad, the situation was quite scary. The entire area looked like a big brown-coloured lake. We took a local person on board and a policeman, so that we don't get lost. As the water levels were quite high, we didn't know whether we were driving our boat along a road or a river, or through a lake. Several times, the bottom of our boat got stuck after hitting the top of totally submerged single-storey bungalows or their gates,' Shabi said.

'We had not seen such big bungalows before. It was a surprise for many of us, the kind of wealth they have,' he mused. The majority of the people rescued from these bungalows by poverty-struck fishermen were relatives of rich Non-Resident Keralites (NRKs), who are the backbone of the state government in terms of the money they remit. According to news reports in February 2018, the deposits by NRKs in Kerala increased by 12 per cent during 2016-17 and stood at Rs 1.5 lakh crores as on March 2017. These figures were borne out by the Economic Review 2017 tabled in the State Assembly as well.

'But when nature was unleashing calamity, the fact is that nothing came to help, other than us. All were on their terraces, drenched in rain with little food for survival and waiting to be rescued,' Shabi said.

*

On the first day itself, Shabi was lucky enough to rescue around 200 people, but it took a severe toll on his health, causing him excruciating neck pain. 'We were told that there were some six men who had been stranded in a two-storey building without food and water for the last two days. We rushed to the spot. But when we reached there, even though we docked our boat on the railings of the second floor, it was quite difficult for them to climb on. As there were strong undercurrents, the boat was also not steady, and they were afraid,' Shabi said. 'We couldn't even tie a rope and haul them onto the boat as they were all heavily built men!'

Finally, Shabi came up with a plan. He stood up in the boat, holding on to the railing, and urged the stranded people to step onto his shoulder and thus climb down into the boat. It worked. All the six stepped on Shabi one by one and climbed down into the boat.

'It was paining like hell for me. I couldn't stop crying. But when I started to think that I have come to save lives, I ignored the pain. I started to believe that the pain from my back is moving to my arm and then into my hand, and finally, disappearing into the air...' Shabi said.

Although his friends on the boat took photos of this, Shabi didn't enjoy the widespread acclaim and rewards that were given to other men who went so far beyond the call of duty or even humanity. For example, a video and photos of Jaisal K.P., a fisherman from Malappuram who offered himself as a footstep to help save lives in Vengara, had gone viral. He had helped elderly women step up into an inflatable boat, winning applause from across the country. A Mahindra showroom in Kerala gifted him a multi-purpose vehicle in recognition of his heroic act. Jaisal was also honoured by Indian National Congress President Rahul Gandhi in Alappuzha. His act of compassion was even featured in the *New York Times*. 'Rescuers use helicopters and even their own backs,' the headline proclaimed, before listing more such 'stories of valor', and describing the fishermen's rescue efforts as 'an Indian Dunkirk'.

Shabi was happy to read about Jaisal and told me that several of the rescuers had done similar things. 'Jaisal's act got noticed. He is lucky. We don't feel disappointed that our acts were not recognized. Jesus knows everything. Even after allowing six people to step on my shoulder, I am okay now. There was pain for a few days. But again, I am back to work. We know that our prayers are heard by Jesus and he will protect us,' he said.

Talking more about his heroic rescue operations,

he recollected how he and his friends rescued twelve women and several small girls from a marooned house.

'One afternoon, while rescuing others, we got a message that twelve women had been stranded in a house across a flooded lake for at least two days. Everyone was afraid of going there because the water in the lake that they had to cross was at a frightening level,' Shabi said. 'We decided to try it anyway.'

It took more than one hour for Shabi and his team to cross the lake as the current was very strong. 'We crossed the lake, but reaching the house was more difficult for us. The house was surrounded by trees. Due to the flow of the water, our boat was losing headway and getting pushed against the trees. So, one of us jumped into the water with a rope that had already been tied to the boat, swam to the tree which was nearest to house and tied the other end to it. After that, we drove the boat forward slowly by holding the rope to guide us,' Shabi said.

When they reached the house, they found another obstacle to overcome. The bottom of the boat got stuck on the gate. They couldn't push the gate open against the weight of the current. Finally, Shabi jumped into the water to see if he could shift the boat. Almost immediately, he saw a snake also in the water nearby.

'The people on the boat started shouting; they were saying that the snake was an extremely venomous one. I was not in any position to get back onto the boat. So I decided to ignore the snake and swim to the gate to see what is causing the block,' Shabi said. 'Luckily, a huge flow of water came and I saw the snake getting swept away from me. When I realized that I am out of danger, I took a dive into the water to see what was blocking the gate. I realized that the gate was locked and couldn't be opened. There were no tools to break the lock. So, we decided to remove the gate from its hooks. Taking a deep breath, one of my friends and I went into that dirty water again. I started removing the mud and my friend tried to lift the gate. After several attempts, we managed to pull out the gate and move it away.'

But the challenges did not end there. They were not able to dock the boat against the second floor of the building, no matter how they tried. Finally, they tied it to a nearby tree. 'It was a few feet away only. If they'd known how to swim or float, they could have reached the boat with our help. But they were all women, so it was not a practical option,' explained Shabi. 'We had to think of an alternative. There were a few banana trees in the compound. We cut them down, chopped off the leaves, tied them together and formed a country-boat.'

Shabi moved the raft to the house, took the young girls on board, and then swam back to his boat by pushing the raft.

'It was okay for the small girls. But I realized that it would be difficult to carry women on the raft. So, we were stuck again. Our only option was to try to tie the boat to the second floor of the house again. It took at least one hour for us to tie the boat to the railings on the second floor, and even then it wasn't steady, being swung around in every direction by the currents in the water. One by one, with a lot of care, we brought the twelve women down into the boat, hoping it would stay still long enough that no one falls in. By then, we all were exhausted and very hungry. It was raining heavily too.' Shabi remembered.

Shabi and his friends had been given food packets by the policemen. But they had saved them to be given to the rescued people when boarding their boat. 'Most of them had remained hungry for at least two or three days. So, we saved our food for them,' Shabi said. 'I saw tears of happiness and thankfulness when they got the food. That inspired us a lot.'

*

Shabi stays in a small house on the shore in Vettucaud. We could see sea waves kissing the shore twenty feet away as we spoke. However, this seemingly idyllic location comes with hazards as dangerous as any he faced while undertaking rescue operations. During the monsoon season, high tides can leave his house marooned. But soon there may be no house at all.

Shabi, who was born and brought up on the shore in this area, remembers that in his school days there was much more shoreland—about 100 feet of land before the sea appeared. 'But it has come down to 10 to 20 feet across the shore. Thousands have lost their houses, and many have taken shelter in the schools. Community leaders say climate change and construction activities are eating up the shore,' Shabi explains.

Beaches along Kerala's 580-kilometre-long coastline face erosion during the South-west monsoon months of May to September and the North-east monsoon between December and January. During these times, high-tide waves drag soil away from the shore. After the monsoon is over, less turbulent waves bring back the eroded sediment and soil. The cyclical process of erosion and accretion should ensure that the beaches remain intact. However, as the sea becomes more and more violent due to climate change and human activities, less and less sediment is returned by the waves, narrowing the width of the beach.

According to Sheeba Patrick, a councillor from the Valiyathura area, about 10 kilometres from Shabi's home, at least 200 houses were damaged during the last year due to high-tide waves. In fact, the high-tide waves of June-July 2018 had razed the office of the National Centre of Earth Science Studies, a government unit set up for the conservation of the environment and management of natural hazards on the shore of Valiyathura.

A report prepared by Dr R.S. Kankara, a scientist at the National Centre for Coastal Research (NCCR), reveals that more than 40 per cent of India's coastal erosion takes place in four states. The report also reveals that almost one-third of India's 6,632-kilometre-long coastline was lost to erosion between 1990 and 2016: West Bengal has already lost 63 per cent of its coastline, Pondicherry 57 per cent, Kerala, 45 per cent and Tamil Nadu, 41 per cent. Quoting M.V. Ramana Murthy, director of the NCCR, *Live Mint* reported that coastal erosion has become a major threat for coastal populations and, without immediate steps taken, 'the damage will be irreversible.' Murthy went on to say, that, 'coastal populations will bear the maximum brunt, especially villages and recent habitations, including buildings, hotels and resorts which are at risk.'

Some residents and climate experts are laying the blame for coastal erosion in Kerala (especially along the Thiruvananthapuram coast) primarily at the feet of man-made ports. 'The construction of a US$65-million international [multi-purpose] port in Vizhinjam is the main reason for shoreline loss around here,' says Joseph Vijayan, a social worker and a petitioner in the case against the port project that is currently being heard by the Supreme Court.

The construction of the port by Adani Ports, India's largest private multi-port operator, began in December 2015 despite stiff resistance from locals and activists. The Vizhinjam Port should be completed by December 2019—but by then, Joseph says, it will be too late. Already, he says, the livelihood of 30,000 residents and fishermen is at stake due to the irreversible ecological damage being caused by the project. 'The construction of a small harbour in Vizhinjam some decades ago caused the shore where I once played football to disappear underwater. If building a small harbour caused that much damage, how much damage will an international port cause?' asks Joseph.

When asked for comment, a senior official from the port, Dr Jayakumar, Managing Director and CEO at Vizhinjam International Seaport Limited, said that 'the erosion in the Thiruvananthapuram coast is not triggered due to the construction of the new port.'

A study conducted by the Centre for Earth Science and Studies (CESS) stated that under the physiographic conditions of Kerala, the population density has tended to increase towards the coastal region. The unstable coastline has not deterred large human settlements near the sea. Out of a total area of 38,863 square kilometres in Kerala, 3,355 fall in coastal regions, supporting a population of over 72 lakh. The density of the coastal urban population is 4,228 per square kilometre, as compared to the average urban density of 2,097 in the state. The coastal rural population density is 1,700, far more than the state's average rural population density of 603 per square kilometre.

'Considering the large number of people, the high concentration of industries, the existence of small and large ports, and the enormous fishing potential, the question of limiting development or putting in place a regime of regulatory measures for human activities on the coast is bound to be highly contentious,' the CESS study concluded.

Meanwhile, the publication of a new draft Coastal Regulation Zone (CRZ) law has also raised serious concerns about the future of India's coastline. Issued by the Ministry of Environment, Forests and Climate Change, the 2018 CRZ notification will make way for more construction on the coast and the easy implementation of several new government ventures which previously failed to get environmental clearances.

One such venture is the multi-billion-dollar Sagarmala mega-project, which will create six new mega ports as well as modernize a few dozen more in various coastal areas across the country. The project was finally adopted in April 2018 and plans to develop at least fourteen Coastal Economic Zones (CEZs) and twenty-nine Coastal Economic Units (CEUs) are currently underfoot. The development of mines, industrial corridors, rail, road and airport connectivity to and from the ports is expected to yield an export revenue growth of US$110 billion. The project is expected to generate over 10 million new jobs by 2025. But activists are concerned that not only will local communities not see any real financial benefit from the project, but that they will also bear the brunt of the environmental degradation it will cause.

A significant modification suggested in the 2018

CRZ draft decreases the buffer zone area from the high-tide line from 500 metres (as in the 2011 draft) to just 50 metres away from the sea. Once in force, the regulation will allow eco-tourism activities such as mangrove walks, tree huts, nature trails, etc in areas very close to the coast through the development of Coastal Zone Management Plans (CZMPs). While no development activities shall be permitted in CRZ-IA areas (classified as the most sensitive coastal zones), the new regulations do not require the setting up of any buffer zone for mangroves located on private land.

According to India's National Fishworkers' Forum General Secretary T. Peter, this spells disaster. 'The new coastal regulations have been drafted only for the easy implementation of the Sagarmala Project that was initially proposed in 2003,' he says, adding that the new CRZ was issued only to help industrialists, especially those in the tourism sector.

Mini Mohan, a social activist, is also fearful of what intensified construction activities on the coast will bring. 'In schools all over the coastal areas, there are shelter camps filled with "sea refugees". We are only going to see more of them if we don't protect the environment,' she said, echoing Shabi's fears.

Sitting with me, looking out onto the sea, Shabi says 'If this situation worsens, one day, we will also lose our house and be forced to move to shelter.'

# 7

## CASTE AND CALLOUSNESS

When Raju Thomas and Arogyadas Ouseph, two fishermen from Marianad, a coastal village in Thiruvananthapuram, volunteered to join rescue operations in Chengannur, among all thoughts of risks, danger and bravery, more mundane issues like caste-based discrimination, earning a living, and government reimbursements were far from their minds.

'When we volunteered to jump into rescue operations, we raised money from our own community. We knew that our boats will be damaged but we didn't think of that loss. We knew that our lives would be at risk in flood waters, but we were ready to lay them down,' Raju said. 'But we couldn't believe that caste could come first for a person whose own life was in danger.'

During the rescue operations in Venmani, a small

village in Chengannur, a group of Brahmin women refused to board their boat. 'The reason they gave was that we belonged to a lower caste and they don't want to become impure by boarding our boat. This was happening when they were in a marooned house!

'We tried our best to convince them that saving their lives comes first. We detailed the risks they took, hoping to reach out to them. A local person with us also tried to persuade them to board our boat. But our pleas were falling on deaf ears. They kept repeating that we are Christians and belong to a lower caste, so travelling with us would contaminate them, make them impure. We had to leave them and move on,' Raju said.

'I can't still understand the logic. We risked our lives. We sacrificed our time. We sacrificed our jobs. At some points, where water levels were low, we had to get down and push the boat to move it forward. After all this, people think that if they board our boat, then they become impure...!'

Fishermen in Kerala come from three different religious groups: Hindu, Muslim and Christian. Hindu fishermen are mostly found in the central and northern districts of Kollam, Alappuzha, Thrissur and Kasargode. They come from the 'Arayan', 'Velan',

'Mukkuva' and 'Marakkan' groups for the most part, all lower-caste groups. Christian and Muslim fishermen are converts from these same Hindu castes, and have been grouped under the 'Dheevaras' category.

Christian fishermen in particular are concentrated in the southern and central parts of Kerala. They belong to the Latin Catholic community and are mostly converts from the Paravar and Mukkuva caste groups. Catholic fishermen are very poor, but are known to be adventurous, aggressive and creative.

According to Raju, the incident has taught them that even though the state and people claim that they are quite progressive, deep inside, Kerala's long history of caste-based discrimination is thriving.

Historians believe that untouchability in Kerala dates to the advent of Namboothiris during the ninth century. Anyone who was not a Namboothiri was treated by the Namboothiris as an untouchable, though they had different rules regarding the degrees of pollution for different castes.

Pollution and impurity rules and their attendant discrimination were practised not only by the Namboothiris, but other communities in Kerala, such as the royal families, temple employees, Nairs, etc. Other South Indian Brahmans also followed these customs for many centuries. Interestingly, in Kerala, the practices around untouchability were not limited to Hindus. Amongst Christians, the original Syrian Malabar Nasranis considered newly converted Latin Christians, usually poorer people and often fishermen, to be untouchables. Many of them also retained a sense of pride in their original Hindu upper-caste identities.

A Nair was expected to instantly cut down a Mukkuvar (fisherman) who presumed to defile him by touching his person; and a similar fate awaited a slave who did not turn out of the road as a Nair passed. According to Kerala's traditions, Dalits were forced to maintain a distance of 24–72 feet from upper-caste people, depending on their particular castes. After Swami Vivekananda, a Hindu monk who was the first person to introduce Indian philosophies of Vedanta and Yoga to the West, toured Malabar (the name for Kerala at the time), in a speech in Chicago in 1887, he said that its residents were 'all lunatics' when it came to caste.

While the extremely rigidly codified practices have largely fallen by the wayside, caste-based discrimination still flourishes. The experiences of Raju and his team reveal that even some 125 years after Vivekananda's speech in Chicago, not a lot has changed. 'Sectarianism, bigotry, and its horrible descendant, fanaticism still exists in Kerala,' Raju said.

*

In contrast, Arogyadas was furious about the self-serving attitudes of the officials on the ground. 'When we finished our two-day-long rescue operations and were readying to return, the officials ignored us. Till then, they needed us. But after that, they showed their true colours,' he recalled.

The fishermen had come for the rescue operations by spending money from their own pockets on hiring trucks and transportation for themselves and their boats. But they expected that the government would support them on their return journeys at least.

'We risked our lives. We swam in filthy water. We drank dirty water and survived on limited food. We carried people on our shoulders. We gave our bodies as steps for them to enter our boats. When the boat was overloaded, we got down and swam with the boat. We rescued pregnant women, new-borns, differently abled, aged and all. We slept on the floor and wore the same wet clothes every day...but when we asked for some fuel, the officials just shooed us away!' Arogyadas said.

According to him, the news claimed that the government had promised free fuel for trucks carrying boats. However, the officials claimed that they didn't have any way to supply or pay for the fuel that the fishermen would need to get themselves and their boats—their livelihoods—home. 'First, they told us that they don't have any clue about such a scheme. We thought that perhaps the officials are unaware, and so we waited for them to check. But there was no word from them at all, and the clock kept ticking. Finally, I had to barge into the officials' room and raise my voice,' Arogyadas said. 'Eventually, the officials said that they would be able to supply only half of what we needed to get home! We were stuck again. We were hungry too, and still exhausted from the rescue attempts. In that condition, we were made to stand for long hours to get a simple answer about the fuel. It was embarrassing and disappointing,' he said, evidently still angry about the callous behaviour of the officials. 'In the end, they agreed to give us coupons so that we could get fuel from petrol pumps on our way back…'

He concluded on a more philosophical note: 'We had been happy to save lives. Our team of twenty boats was able to rescue more than 4,000 stranded people from marooned houses. We'd volunteered for that only. So, in the end, these red tape hassles are not going to make us worry. Yes, it was disappointing. But we have decided to ignore such disappointments!'

# 8

## IT WAS A LESSON FOR US...
## AND FOR THEM TOO

Vino B., Shelton G. and Johnas F., all in their late thirties, are not regular sea-goers. But, as members of fisher families in Vizhinjam, they have been to sea once in a while and they own a boat. It is often rented to others from their own hamlet for fishing. They run a workshop for boat engines on the coast near the village. 'We can be called fishermen and mechanics too,' Vino said.

However, not being regular sea-goers didn't stop them from wanting to jump into flood rescue operations and giving whatever help they could. They were ready with their boat loaded onto a truck, when they found that they weren't on the list of nineteen teams arranged from their area by the Church. After waiting for a long day, the trio had decided to drop their plan to join the rescue operations. It was then that they got a call from someone in an Arabian country, seeking their help for relatives in Changanassery, a central Travancore town, badly hit by the floods.

*

During the floods, many Keralites in the Gulf Consortium Countries (GCC, or simply the Gulf) had been frantically making calls and posting on social media, seeking help for their near and dear ones who were stranded, alone and without any chance of family coming to their rescue. Those who work in the Gulf are often not in a position to get emergency leave. Even if a close relative passes away, migrant workers from Kerala have to wait a minimum of forty-eight hours to process the paperwork for leave and get an exit permit from the Gulf.

Due to the exploitative employment conditions, the reality is much worse. The majority of the migrant workers in the region have to follow the Kafala system, which restricts the free movement of the worker. A 'sponsorship system,' the Kafala ties the legal residency of workers to their employers. It emerged in the 1950s to regulate the relationship between employers and migrant workers in many countries in West Asia.

The sponsorship system's economic objective was to provide temporary, rotating labour that could be rapidly brought into the country at times of economic boom and expelled during less affluent periods. It still remains the routine practice in the Gulf and in the Arab states of Jordan and Lebanon.

Under the Kafala system a migrant worker's immigration status is legally bound to an individual employer or sponsor (kafeel) for their contract period. The migrant worker cannot enter the country, transfer employment or leave the country for any reason without first obtaining explicit written permission from the kafeel. The kafeel must report to the immigration authorities if the migrant worker leaves their employment and must ensure that the worker leaves the country after the contract ends, including paying for the flight home. Often, the kafeel exerts further control over migrant workers by confiscating their passport and travel documents, despite legislation in some destination countries that declares this practice illegal. This situates the migrant worker as completely dependent upon their kafeel for their livelihood and residency.

The kafeel's labour needs are met in the context of immense control and unchecked leverage over workers, creating an environment ripe for human rights violations and erosion of labour standards. The power that the Kafala system delegates to the sponsor over the migrant worker has been likened to a contemporary form of slavery.

Inherent in the Kafala system is the assumption that workers are considered temporary contract labour, reflected in in the GCC's official use of 'guest workers' and 'expatriate manpower' to refer to migrant workers. Even if the worker is present for a long time s/he cannot acquire the rights of citizenship, due to its alleged negative impact on the social cohesiveness of the destination country.

The restrictive immigration policies of the Kafala system act in theory to limit the stay of overseas workers to the duration of their contract. However, non-compliance by both employers and migrant workers in response to the demand for labour has led to a sizeable minority of long-term or permanent residents, along with a significant number of second-generation migrants and the development of irregular employment. Thus, migrant workers may remain for years, vulnerable to the threat of unpaid wages, arrest, detention and ultimately deportation, should they complain or leave.

If the migrant worker decides to leave the workplace without the employer's written consent, they may be charged with 'absconding', which is a criminal offense. Even if a worker leaves in response to abuse, they remain at risk of being treated as a criminal rather than receiving appropriate victim support. Often, s/he simply cannot leave, since the employer has possession of her/his passport.

The Kafala system affects 23 million migrant workers across the Middle East, where many are trapped in slave-like conditions. Some isolated cases of easy access to an exit permit or leave approval exist for migrant workers in top level management, but the majority of the mid- and low-level workers have to wait for the benevolence of the employer, even for an emergency leave.

The majority of the people of Chengannur are in the Gulf, Europe and the Americas. Unfortunately, while the younger generation are working in the foreign lands, their aged parents are left behind to live alone in Chengannur. Due to the employment systems and high airfares, they visit their parents once a year, or sometimes even once in two or three years, usually during Onam, Kerala's harvest festival, or Christmas. These are the times when aged parents meet their children and grandchildren. It is only then that it is possible to tell that somebody lives in these huge gated villas, situated in lonely splendour in the centre of a big garden, far from the main road.

*

Vino B., Shelton G. and Johnas F. reached the big houses of Changanassery early in the morning.

'We didn't think twice after the phone call. Without informing the Church, we took our truck and left for Changanassery. We had a little money with us, so we bought fuel and stocked up. We were aware that as we were not listed in the Church's team, we wouldn't get any facilities from the government,' Vino said.

Those who registered their names with the government before taking part in the rescue operations were supposed to be given some fuel, food and life jackets. However, there were allegations that a few registered fishermen also had to fight to get the government's facilities. In any case, the majority of the fishermen who registered didn't stand in queues to collect the items due to them. They just jumped into action as they realized that the water level was rising.

Shelton and his team did the same kind of rescue work as the other fishermen. They rescued children, aged people, physically challenged patients, pregnant women and toddlers.

'Rescuing some people was risky, while others were easy. We had to really risk our lives when we dived into the flood water or climbed slippery slopes to the second floors. We fell many times. But we didn't hurt anyone whom we had rescued,' Shelton said.

'In addition to saving some 400 lives in two days, which we see as a great achievement in our life, we learnt a great lesson. It was a lesson for those who were rescued also,' Johnas said.

The universal truth is that money doesn't help at all times.

'We were told about a marooned house and aged parents stranded in a huge gated villa. The villa was surrounded by huge trees, so the Navy choppers had not been able to land on the terrace. We were told to head there and try to see whether we could rescue them or not,' Shelton said.

When Shelton and his team reached the villa, it was quite risky for them to dock their boat. 'Even though we tied the boat to the railings of the second floor, a strong undercurrent kept shaking it. Two of us had to get down from the boat into the flood water and hold it to keep it stable. The third person went into the house and brought the elderly couple to the boat,' Shelton said.

'They had not had food for the last two days. Whatever reserves they had were over. So we shared the food packets given to us. We realized how hungry they were when we saw the way they were eating,' he added.

After eating, they told us that a chopper had come to rescue them three separate times. But as it couldn't land any of the times, they had had to abort the mission.

Shelton quoted the elderly couple's words to the trio: 'We have enough money to hire or even buy a chopper. But at this time, that money didn't come to help. It's you people, whom we have not met earlier, who came to help. This is a lesson for us. Money can't buy everything and it can't come to help when we are in dire straits. We have realized that. That's a great lesson.'

And Shelton added that it was a great lesson for the three of them too. 'We were not told by anybody to join the rescue team. We did it ourselves. We didn't know the people whom we rescued. We are not going to see them again either. They may forget us. We may forget them. But the lesson we learnt won't be forgotten. We suffered Rs 50,000 worth of damage to our boat and its engine. But we are not going to claim it. We saved around 400 lives and learnt a big lesson too. That's enough for this life.

'Do all get a chance to save people's lives...? No,' Shelton concluded.

It's true that only a few, like Shelton, are blessed to save lives. Ordinary people like you and me are not.

# 9

## WE DID WHAT THE NAVY AND
## ARMY COULDN'T

Till now, we've read about the heroism of young fishermen. We read how they dived into muddy flood waters, broke open gates underwater to make way for their boats, picked venomous snakes up in their naked hands, slid down from rooftops with a rescued person tied onto their body directly into the boat, drove the boat without any safety gear, ignored hunger and thirst for hours in the rush to save lives, risked their own lives, forgot their near and dear ones back home... And now we hear about a veteran who did all that the youngsters did, despite being in his late fifties.

Wilfred S., a veteran fisherman from Vizhinjam in Thiruvananthapuram, who saved around 500 people from the worst flood-hit area on the banks of the Pamba river, was the only elder among the rescuers.

When asked why he decided to rescue people whom he didn't know, risking his life at this age, Wilfred had an immediate answer: 'If not I, who else will do it? And, moreover, what is special about this? I see it as my duty. I used my experience in fighting the rough sea, skills of steering the boat, and the courage given by Jesus Christ. That's it...'

Wilfred had a rich experience of fishing life to share. And when he started to tell his personal story of struggle, poverty, starvation, fight for survival, family, children, his own hamlet...he unknowingly told different chapters from every fisherman's life of the past five decades.

'At the age of ten, I started to go into the deep sea with my father on an ordinary catamaran. Those days, there were no engine-driven catamarans or boats like now. We had to "steer" the boat by pulling the ropes of tarpaulin according to the wind's direction. We were never afraid of the killer waves. Sometimes we used to fall and sometimes, we used to get lost in the sea too. But the prayers of our loved ones on the shore would bring us back with a good catch,' Wilfred said.

'Our families could only have something to eat when we returned to sell the fish we'd caught, and buy rice. During those days, there were no gas stoves anywhere in our hamlet. So, if we saw smoke coming from one of the houses, it was a happy sign. We'd know that they were not starving, and we could also ask them for some food. There was a lot of sharing and caring among us in those days. We starved together and ate together.'

Wilfred feels that those good days have gone and now, the majority of the youngsters in the hamlet lead an irresponsible life. 'Now, they go fishing on boats with double engines. Most of the time they return with a good catch. But they fail to take care of their family. I can say that there are mainly three type of people in the coastal areas. Some earn and spend everything on booze. The number of these people is huge. The second type spend half of what they earn for booze and give the rest to their family. And the third take good care of their family. But their number is too low. The majority lead an irresponsible life without any thought of the future. They don't want to progress, nor do they want their children to lead a good and decent life,' Wilfred concluded.

*

According to Wilfred, the majority of the fishermen don't go to church any more. 'They are less interested in those kinds of needs. It's very rare that they come to Church, be a God-fearing person and lead a moral life.'

The Church has played a vital role in the lives of fishermen in south Kerala, especially in the Travancore area. History books reveal that when Christianity came to Kerala, Travancore was a staunchly Hindu princely state where each community had its own customs and conventions. They worshipped many gods and goddesses.

According to researchers in Thiruvananthapuram, Christianity in Kerala is as old as Christianity itself, and Kerala is rightly called the cradle of Christianity in India. Quoting Church records, they claim that many Keralites had become Christians even before St Peter reached Rome in 68 AD. Kerala Christians have a longer history and a more ancient ancestry than the Christians of most European countries. Even when European missionaries first landed in Kerala, they found that there were several Christian strongholds here.

Before being converted to Christianity, the fishermen in Travancore and the southern tip of Tamil Nadu, especially Kanyakumari and nearby areas, belonged to the Paravar community, a Tamil Hindu caste.

The Paravars were coastal inhabitants, pearl divers, seafarers, maritime traders and subordinate rulers to the Pandyas. The current name for them, Mukkuva, is said to have evolved from Muthu Varunnavar (pearl collectors).

If we jump to 1527, we see that the Paravars were being threatened by Arab fleets offshore and also by an onshore campaign by the Rajah of Madura to wrest control of Tirunelveli. This continuing situation, and the desire to be relieved of rivalry from the Lebbai, the Tamil Muslim pearl divers, caused the Paravars to seek the protection of Portuguese explorers who had moved into the area.

A delegation headed by Vikirama Aditha Pandya visited Goa for talks to this end in 1532. The protection was granted on the condition that the leaders would immediately be baptized as Catholics and that they would encourage their people also to convert to Catholicism. The Portuguese would also gain a strategic foothold on the Indian coast and control of the lucrative pearl fisheries.

Some months later, 20,000 Paravars were baptized en masse, and became subjects of Portugal. By the end of 1537 the entire community had declared itself to be Catholics and the Portuguese proceeded to destroy the Arab fleet when they met fortuitously at Vedalai on 27 June 1538.

From that point onwards, the Paravar people as a whole enjoyed renewed prosperity. Their declaration of acceptance of the Catholic faith did not prevent them from continuing to worship in the manner they had done previously, because there were no translators to spread the Catholic message and also because the conversion was seen by the Paravar people as being merely a convenient arrangement to obtain protection, not a statement of belief.

Meanwhile, Francis Xavier, a Jesuit priest and one of the greatest preachers, had been working in Goa prior to his journey to Kanyakumari. Xavier had been appointed at the earnest solicitation of John III, King of Portugal, to evangelize the people of the East Indies. He had left Rome on March 16, 1540 and landed at Goa on May 6, 1542. There, he spent the first five months in preaching and ministering to the sick in the hospitals. According to Fr Errol Fernandes SJ in his book *Beyond Frontiers and Boundaries,* Francis Xavier would go through the streets ringing a little bell and inviting children to hear the word of God.

In about October 1542, he started for the pearl

fisheries of the extreme southern coast of the peninsula, desirous of restoring Christianity which, although introduced years before, had almost disappeared due to the lack of priests. He devoted almost three years to the work of preaching to the people of Western India, converting many, and reaching even Sri Lanka.

During the visit of Xavier, the Vadugars or the Vijayanagar forces attacked Travancore. Their raids had become a sort of annual ritual. But in 1542, Xavier helped the king to drive the Vijayanagar forces away and saved the kingdom. As a token of love and good faith, Xavier was permitted to propagate Christianity.

Churches were established in Poovar, Kollancodu, Vallavizhai, Thoothoor, Poothurai, Thengapattanam, Enayam, Midalam, Vanniyakudi, Colachel, Kadiapattanam, Muttom and Pallam. Xavier made Kottar the main centre because it was already an important town for the Venad Kingdom. Historians claim that a further 10,000 Paravars were baptized during the first month of his mission, and 30,000 in total by its end.

Before leaving the area, Xavier appointed catechists in the Paravar villages all along the coastline, to spread his teachings and make sure that they were remembered. After this, he went on to travel through Southeast Asia, before returning eventually to Goa, where he was buried.

Vikirama Aditha Pandya was rewarded by the Portuguese for his actions of 1532 when, as part of the arrangement for protection, he had offered to manage the pearl diving on their behalf. He became known as Senhor dos Senhores ('first among notables') Dom João da Cruz and was recognized as headman and official intermediary by the Portuguese from 1543 until 1553.

Today also, along the coast, the Church has the final word when it comes to the important decisions of fishermen's lives. As a recent example, when Cyclone Ockhi struck the Thiruvananthapuram and Kanyakumari coast in 2017, it was the Church and the priests who coordinated the rescue operations, negotiated terms with the state and central government, and assisted the rehabilitation of the cyclone's victims.

Wilfred was among the fishermen who assisted the Indian Navy in its rescue operations at the time of Cyclone Ockhi.

*

'Many had gone deep sea fishing from the coast of Thiruvananthapuram and Kanyakumari. As there was some confusion in the alerts, they were not aware of the cyclone and eventually got stranded in the rough seas,' Wilfred said.

Hundreds of fishermen who had gone fishing without any knowledge of the arriving cyclone had gone missing. Their disappearance forced the fishermen's community to initiate their own rescue operations.

There were allegations that the Coast Guard and the Indian Navy were reluctant to bring back bodies and also to widen their search beyond a certain nautical radius.

'We had told them from the first day to take our assistance. But they were reluctant... Finally, they agreed. But by then it was too late,' Wilfred said. 'It happened only after the Church had put immense pressure on the government to take us to the sea along with the government rescue teams, to save lives. Many who went, like me, were able to locate bodies and it was evident that we were arriving too late,' Wilfred said.

Fishermen claimed that if they had been taken for the rescue operations from the first day itself, they could have saved many lives.

In December 2018, Defence Minister Nirmala

Sitharaman informed Parliament that a total of 661 fishermen continued to remain missing in the aftermath of Cyclone Ockhi. She said that 400 fishermen were missing from Tamil Nadu and 261 from Kerala. In the rescue operations carried out by the Indian Navy, Indian Coast Guard and the Indian Air Force, 821 fishermen were rescued. Other agencies, including merchant vessels and trawlers, rescued twenty-four people. Among the fishermen saved, 453 were from Tamil Nadu, 362 from Kerala and thirty from the Lakshadweep and Minicoy islands.

*

While talking about his exploits during the 2018 flood rescue operations, I asked Wilfred why he took such risks at his age. He just smiled and answered that he doesn't know why he went. But he doesn't regret that decision.

'From the age of ten, I have been taking risks, and I am used to it. My family also knows that. They have seen that. In our earlier days, even going for fishing was a risk. It was not guaranteed that we would come back. So, when I decided to join the flood rescue operations, I and my family were not worried,' Wilfred said.

Wilfred was part of a nineteen boat team which went from Vizhinjam under the guidance of the Church. 'When the flood water was rising in Central Travancore and the government wanted us to rescue lives, we didn't hesitate. I saw that it was all youngsters, but I knew that my experience as a sailor would help,' he added.

Wilfred and his team went to the Kuttanad area which was totally submerged in the floods. 'When we reached there, it was like we are in the middle of sea. The only difference is that the sea is relatively calm when compared to the wildly flowing flood water,' Wilfred added.

In forty-eight hours, Wilfred and his team were able to rescue some 400 stranded people. Most of the rescued people were elderly or physically challenged or women. 'In those areas, men work abroad. And their parents were left alone in big houses. The challenge was that they all were aged, heavily built and suffering from many diseases. This increased our risk. We had to spend a lot of time to convince them that they will be safe in our hands and we can take them to shelters,' Wilfred explained.

Just like the youngsters in the team, Wilfred also swam in the flood waters, moved the heavy gates, took many on his shoulders, and steered the boat out from dangers.

Once, when the boat was about to turn upside down while it had rescued people on board, Wilfred caught hold of a power supply line to hold the boat straight. When asked why he made such a rash decision, he said that he was sure that power supply in the area was cut off due to the floods and, in any case, other than holding onto the power supply line, there were no other options. 'If I hadn't done that, the boat would have turned upside down in the heavily flowing flood water, and the rescued people would have drowned, which would have been a tragedy,' Wilfred said.

*

'After two days of tiring rescue operations, ignoring hunger and danger, we decided to end our task. We loaded our boat on the truck and were ready to go. We were waiting to sign some official papers with the government officials about the rescue operations, when there came a request from the government,' Wilfred said.

'They asked us to transport some food and medicines to about 350 people who had taken shelter on a small hilltop across the Pamba river. All of them were from nearby areas. When the flood water had started to rise, they had moved to the hilltop so that at least they would have saved their lives. As the hilltop was full of trees, the Navy and Army choppers had failed to drop medicines and food for the stranded people and they had been literally starving for at least three days.

'The time was around six p.m. We were aware that by the time we reached, it would be dark. However, we decided to go.' It was also raining heavily. 'Without any delay, we unloaded the boat from the truck. The officials and volunteers loaded the medicines and food. A local who knows the way also joined us,' Wilfred said.

According to Wilfred, it was a risky task. To reach the spot, he and his team would have had to cross the Kuttanad lake and the ferociously flowing Pamba. 'The water level in the lake was quite high. As we had to be more cautious, we were driving the boat a little slowly. Crossing the lake itself took more than one hour. And by then the light was disappearing. Somehow, we entered the Pamba river. The river was flowing at its full. Even the sight of its flow was scary. We had to drive in the opposite direction, against the current, which, again, was a risky job—and time consuming too. As it's a river that flows down from the hills, there were uprooted trees and many other floating objects coming down, threatening to capsize us. To avoid a head-on crash, we had to divert the boat many times. Finally, after a two-hour drive, we reached the destination.'

When Wilfred docked their boat and climbed the hilltop with medicine and food, the stranded people were really surprised to see them. 'More than getting the medicines and food, they were happy to learn that the government was aware of them and hadn't given up on them,' he said.

Wilfred and his team could only spend a few minutes with them as it was becoming dark very quickly. 'Returning was riskier. Now, we had to drive along with the flow of river. So, most of the time we were losing control. We were thrown up and down many times by the river. At one time, we even thought that we would all fall into the water and drown. But somehow, we reached the shelter,' Wilfred said.

Upon reaching the shelter, Wilfred and his team were given a hero's welcome by the officials and volunteers as they hadn't been sure that they would be able to complete the mission successfully where the well-trained Navy and Army personnel with their choppers had failed.

'By going to the rescue operations, what we could do is help people with our limited resources. We believed in our experience of braving the killer waves in the sea. That helped us a lot,' Wilfred concluded.

# APPENDIX

# A HISTORY OF HEROISM

While speaking to the fishermen of the Thiruvananthapuram coast in their own homes and hamlets, I heard many refer to their long history of courage and daring. When pressed for specifics, most of them could only give vague stories, passed on through the generations, but they were all clear that their legacy shows that they have ignored risks to save others' lives and protect their nation in the past. On this basis, they say, they continue to do so now, and will in the future as well.

Intrigued, and wanting to know more about this history, I contacted Father Antony Claret, a priest from the fisherfolk community himself, who has been researching about his community from the Chinnavilai Church, Manavalaikurichi, a town near Colachel, at the southern tip of Tamil Nadu. In fact, he has written a book on the Colachel War of 1741 in Tamil, drawing on extensive research, and particularly focusing on a book, *The Kulasekhara Perumals of Travancore: History and State Formation in Travancore from 1671 to 1758* written by Mark Erik Jan de Lannoy.

\*

If it hadn't been for the fisherfolk community of old Travancore in the eighteenth century, the famed ruler Marthanda Varma would perhaps have lost his kingdom to the Dutch forces, says Fr Antony Claret. Born Anizham Thirunal Marthanda Varma in 1705, and fondly called Marthanda Varma by his subjects, he was the ruler of Travancore from 1729 until his death in 1758. 'Marthanda Varma is most celebrated for defeating the Dutch expansionist designs at the Battle of Colachel in 1741. And when we refer to some of the historical books, eyewitness accounts and recorded testimonies about the war, we see that the fishermen along the coast had played a vital role in helping the King of Travancore,' explained Fr Claret. He said that they helped him stop Dutch invasions three times.

According to history books, the Travancore–Dutch War was a war between the Dutch East India Company and Travancore, culminating in the Battle of Colachel in 1741. The seeds of the war were sowed when Marthanda Varma began expanding his kingdom by entering into territorial disputes with his neighbours, the Kingdoms of Kayamkulam and Kollam in 1731. These disputes began impacting the Dutch East India Company since they had established factories for processing and exporting pepper in these areas, collectively known as Dutch Malabar. By 1733, the Dutch East India Company's pepper exports had dropped to less than half the quantities of 1730-31. The advent of British traders in this market had also made the price of pepper soar.

To help the three kingdoms mediate their differences, the Dutch East India Company first deputed their emissaries, William Feling, Abraham van de Welle, Ezechiel Rhabbi and Brouwer to Kayamkulam in May 1734 to negotiate with Marthanda Varma. However, they were unsuccessful and three years later, Marthanda Varma's annexation of Eleyadathu Swarupam, the largest pepper producing area in southern Kerala, made a confrontation between him and the Dutch East India Company inevitable.

As part of his expansion plans, Marthanda Varma had crushed the opposition to his rule in Travancore and then absorbed the kingdom of Attingal. His next target was Quilon, currently known as Kollam, whose ruler was Unni Kerala Varma. He was an ally of Kayamkulam. The King of Kayamkulam had formed an alliance with the rulers of Cochin, Purakkad and Vadakkumkur against Marthanda Varma.

In 1739, Marthanda Varma refused to recognize the claim of the senior princess of the Kottarakara family to the succession, following the death of the chief of the Elayadathu Swarupam. She, in turn, appealed to the Dutch East India Company. The Dutch were unhappy with the annexation of the kingdoms of their allies and a meeting between Marthanda Varma and the Dutch factor van Imhoff aggravated the situation, with van Imhoff threatening to attack Venad and Marthanda Varma threatening to carry war into Dutch territories.

In 1741, the Dutch formally installed the princess as the ruler of Kottarakara. A combined Kottarakara-Dutch army was decisively defeated by Marthanda Varma's army and the state of Kottarakara was annexed. Marthanda Varma then also captured the Dutch forts in the vicinity. All of this forced the Dutch East India Company to engage Marthanda Varma and thus began the Travancore–Dutch war that led to the Battle of Colachel.

'When the Dutch Navy was nearing the coast, the

fishermen in the Colachel area placed palm trees on stones to look like canons. In addition, some of the fishermen stood along the beach in multiple rows with oars kept along their shoulders so that they would appear like soldiers standing with their guns. This frightened the Dutch Navy,' Fr Claret said.

A Dutch force under the command of De Lennoy landed at Colachel from Cochin and captured the country up to Kottar. Marthanda Varma marched south and prevented the capture of Kalkulam by the Dutch. When the Dutch retreated to their base in Colachel, Marthanda Varma pursued them.

'The second time, the Dutch employed a fisherman from the coast and wanted to use his boat to transport one of their officials to Kanyakumari,' Fr Claret said. The Dutch official was supposed to go to Kanyakumari to bring in more reinforcements to Colachel to fight the war. 'But the fisherman took a detour. He rowed the boat to Colachel instead of Kanyakumari, and eventually, handed over the senior Dutch official to Marthanda Varma.'

The Dutch still continued to hope for reinforcements from Kanyakumari, as they were rapidly running out of ammunition. 'But the fishermen were not ready to bring their boats and ships to Colachel. It was the

South-west monsoon season. The sea was rough. But mainly, we can see that the fishermen were reluctant to lead the reinforcement supply boats to the struggling Dutch Navy,' explains Fr Claret.

These three actions of the fishermen played a vital role in the defeat of the Dutch, along with their own corruption which led to the shoddy building of the Dutch fort in Colachel. Marthanda Varma's army easily blasted it open. With the battle of Colachel, Marthanda Varma won a decisive victory over the Dutch. A pillar of victory which gives details about the war still stands near the coast of Colachel.

In the words of the noted historian, Prof. Sreedhara Menon, 'A disaster of the first magnitude for the Dutch, the battle of Colachel shattered for all time their dream of the conquest of Kerala.' Despite allying with the enemies of Travancore in subsequent battles, right up to the battle of Ambalapuzha (1756), the battle of Colachel was a death blow to the power of the Dutch East India company in the Malabar coast. In addition to the destruction of the Dutch East India Company's designs in the Malabar coast, the capture of the leader of the expedition, de Lannoy, was very beneficial to the Kingdom of Travancore. He took up service with Travancore and modernized the Travancore Army into an effective fighting force, using better artillery, modern firearms and, most importantly, the European style of military drill and tactics. This army went on to conquer more than half of Kerala, and the forts de Lannoy had designed held up to the advance of Tipu Sultan's army during the Third Anglo-Mysore War in 1791.

*

The local fishermen, who were Paravars—a lower Hindu caste—had been converted to Catholicism by Francis Xavier in the sixteenth century. They had been instrumental in helping the King of Travancore at the time to defeat the long-running menace of the annual Pandya raids.

'Usually, Vadugas, a clan from Pandya Kingdom, used to collect tax from Travancore. Most of the time, the Travancore rulers would fail to collect the tax and the Vadugas would do an annual raid. During the raid they used to loot Travancore,' explained Fr Claret. 'But this time, they were stopped by Fr Xavier. He used the help of the local fishermen to do so. We can infer that the fishermen were brave, loyal and ready to take risks,' he said, adding that the modern fishermen had displayed the same characteristcs while rescuing people from flood-hit areas in Kerala.

According to historians, as a reward in return, the King of Travancore at the time facilitated Francis Xavier in his missionary activities, thereby ensuring that the fisherfolk community of the Kerala coast remained largely Catholic, right up to the present.

*

When I asked him about the history of the fishermen, the general secretary of the National Fishworkers' Forum, Peter T., said that fishermen have bravery in their blood. To portray how willing they are to disregard risk, he told me a story:

'Most of the time, when confrontation happens between us [unions] and the police, they fire warnings in the air to disperse the protestors. But we fishermen don't realize that it is meant to be a warning,' he said. 'This has happened in the past several times. Whenever the police would fire in the air, we would be unaffected, and walk forward. When the police saw our unshaken protest, they would finally fire directly at us and some of us would lose our lives...'

Coming back to the floods of 2018, he explained: 'Fishermen also risk their life to protect others. That's what we saw during the flood. Even before the government and the Church called fishermen to volunteer for rescue operations, they jumped into action. On 670 boats, they rescued 65,000 people. This number is about ten times more than the number of people rescued by the Army and Navy!'

It is clear that whatever the reasons, the bravery of the fishermen and their selflessness in putting themselves at risk for people they'd never met was amply demonstrated in 2018. Their courageous deeds should be celebrated all over the world.

# ACKNOWLEDGEMENTS

I could not have written this book without the help of my loving wife, Karthika Reji. Being a chronic insulin-dependent diabetic, my moods swing a lot and I often quickly fall into depression. Travelling all along the coastal areas on my 350cc motorbike to write this book weakened me physically as well. But she stood with me throughout, making sure that I manage everything, whether hyperglycaemia, medicines or moods. She would set alarms to wake me every morning to write. More than thanking her, I would like the world to know that this book could not have happened if she had not stood with me.

I should also thank my caring mother, Remani K.K., who helps me to fight the odds even though I'm in my forties now. I am glad for my children, nine-year-old Rishikesh Reji, and seven-year-old Kasinath Reji, who were ready to skip their outings when I had to travel to fishing hamlets far away from home for this book. And, of course, my sister, Rekha K., who always valued all my works and takes pride in me.

Apart from my family, I should thank Dr Shashi Tharoor, the parliamentarian from Thiruvananthapuram, who has sent this book as part of the documentary evidence for his Nobel Peace Prize recommendation for these brave fishermen.

I can't miss thanking my colleague Mini Mohan, who worked from the beginning of the book with me. She helped in connecting me with these brave fishermen and guiding me to capture the true stories from fishing villages in the coastal areas, as well as the flood-hit areas in central Travancore.

Of course, there is a long list of friends too. Its impracticable to list them all here. However, this acknowledgment will be incomplete without mentioning V.S. Pramod, my friend from school, who now works in a regional language newspaper in Kerala. He was always impressed with my ideas, while also at the same time critical in correcting them for this book. In fact, it was Pramod who travelled with me to southern Tamil Nadu, hunting for the histories of the brave fisherfolk of the coastal area.

I should also thank Huberston Tomwilson, a lawyer in southern Tamil Nadu, who took me to the right person who had documented local history, and Crystal Ennis, a friend and lecturer in Leiden University in the Netherlands, who browsed the entire university library in search of a thesis paper which mentioned the part fisherfolk communities played in Dutch history for me. I would also like to thank Fr Eugene H. Pereira from Thiruvananthapuram Archdiocese for introducing me to researchers while I was exploring these histories.

I would like to thank Joe A. Scaria, a former editor with *The Economic Times* and my teacher in journalism school, who has always been appreciative of my writing.

I should also thank Shalini Krishan, editor with Speaking Tiger, who was impressed with my book idea and without whom this book would not have come out in this way.

I must thank Mustafa Qadri, Executive Director of Equidem Research and Consulting, for providing me support and adjusting my schedule to enable me to write this book alongside my regular work.

Finally, and most importantly, I must thank all my brave fishermen friends along the Thiruvananthapuram coast, especially Saju Antony, Jack Mandalo and Johny Chekkitta, not least for introducing me to other groups of fishermen and having the conversations that make up this book.

Obliged.

Rejimon Kuttappan
Thiruvananthapuram
July 2019

www.ingramcontent.com/pod-product-compliance
Lightning Source LLC
Chambersburg PA
CBHW070345270326
41926CB00017B/3991